F

i

ENDURING VALUES

Media and Society Series

J. Fred MacDonald, *General Editor*

ENDURING VALUES

Women in Popular Culture

June Sochen

PRAEGER

New York
Westport, Connecticut
London

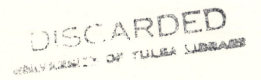

Library of Congress Cataloging-in-Publication Data

Sochen, June, 1937-
  Enduring values.

  (Media and society series)
  Bibliography: p.
  Includes index.
  1. Women in popular culture—United States—History—
20th century. 2. Women in mass media—United States—
History—20th century. 3. Social values—History—20th
century. I. Title. II. Series.
HQ1420.S58   1987   305.4'2'0973   87-15158
ISBN 0-275-92739-3 (alk. paper)

Library of Congress Catalog Card Number: 87-15158
ISBN: 0-275-92739-3

First published in 1987

Praeger Publishers, One Madison Avenue, New York, NY 10010
A division of Greenwood Press, Inc.

Printed in the United States of America

The paper used in this book complies with the
Permanent Paper Standard issued by the National
Information Standards Organization (Z39.48-1984).

10 9 8 7 6 5 4 3 2 1

To Julie, Sarina, Abby, and Adam Schrager

Contents

Preface

This book is a detailed discussion of twentieth century popular cultural treatments of women (with one foray into an analysis of nineteenth century women writers). It is largely devoted to U.S. women performers in popular music, movies, and television, the mass media I consider the most important in shaping values and images of women. This book looks at both women practitioners and performers in the respective fields studied as well as the dominant images conveyed by their portrayals. The enormously popular women stars often confirmed majority attitudes about women. On the other hand, some successful entertainers such as Eva Tanguay at the beginning of the century and Bette Midler near the end of the century projected unusual images of women; they were the rebels, the outsiders, who flaunted society's views on women to the love of their audiences.

Another major concern of *Enduring Values* is how deeply held cultural values that shaped our views of women are reflected in popular culture. It is suggestive in its interpretation and offers readers both information on forgotten stars and ideas about popular culture that have application to contemporary life. It is both a historical look at the twentieth century, though a very selective one, and a current analysis of women's images and women performers. It offers a framework within which readers can view television programs, listen to the lyrics of popular songs, or watch a movie.

It provides the reader with interpretive views to investigate other stars as well as to determine how relevant the images discussed still are.

As in every enterprise, many people have encouraged and aided me in my work. I am very grateful to my students at Northeastern Illinois University (UNI), whose papers and comments in my two courses on the subject, Women in Popular Culture and Women in Film, have been invaluable; to my colleague, Fred MacDonald, who has generously shared his impressive popular cultural holdings with me and whose editorial advice has been extremely helpful; to Flo Levy, Agnes Rodriguez, and Helene Rogers, UNI History Department secretaries for their typing of earlier drafts of the manuscript; and to my family, who are always a lively inspiration to me. This book is dedicated to my favorite members of the younger generation, my nieces and nephew: Julie, Sarina, Abby, and Adam Schrager. Ultimately, of course, the opinions in this book are my own, for which I assume full responsibility.

Introduction

The popular culture of the United States contains both new and old elements; it searches constantly for new stars, new plots, and new twists while remaining true to old images, old formulas, and old values. Nowhere is this more clearly seen than in its depiction of women—old images presented in new packagings. Indeed, there have been durable, dominant images of women throughout U.S. cultural history, both in its elite and popular forms. First in literature and then, in the twentieth century, in the electronic media, women have been portrayed as three basic types: as Mary, Eve, and independent woman. Using biblical characters as the basis for the imagery of Mary and Eve especially, their features become easily apparent.

Mary has appeared in all cultural formulas as the good, virginal woman, vulnerable and in need of a male's protection and support. Even when she was a married woman, she was depicted as pure, submissive, and good. Eve, the sexual temptress, is the beautiful, alluring woman who uses her sexuality to tempt males into sin and excitement. Because she is the evil woman, Eve is usually punished by our conventional culture at the end of the story. The independent woman is the most unusual; she is strong, distinctive, and self-possessed; while she rarely appeared in the Bible (except in the mythic story of Lilith), she has achieved some popularity in U.S. popular culture. All three images contain essential female and human traits.

The independent woman has appeared in U.S. cultural imagery during periods of stress, such as the Great Depression, and in periods of women's liberation, such as the 1960s. *Enduring Values* focuses upon the multiple expressions of the independent woman image since it is the most exciting and various. It is the least predictable and appears in most of the popular formulas—in romance, comedy, melodrama, and adventure. Sometimes, the independent woman combines Eve-like or Mary-like qualities into her persona, while strength and individuality remain her essential ingredients. The independent woman may be a careerist, an aristocratic lady whose financial independence gives her the opportunity to live her own life, or she may be an Independent Eve who has to overcome difficult circumstances on her own. But she is always a survivor in an often hostile environment.

All women embody some of the characteristics of the three images. All women have strengths, sexual natures, and moral character. Women also dream of possessing the ideal: of being perfect examples of beauty, purity, and independence. This is precisely why these three images have remained such powerful conveyors of women's nature. In the realm of popular culture, of course, sometimes the expressions are simpleminded, one-dimensional, and distorted. When that is the case, they are examples of bad stereotyping; when the woman's part in a melodrama, for example, captures authentic dimensions of any of the three images, the portrait draws closer to the ideal image.

The relationship between women's image and its treatment in popular culture is a complex one. It is rarely a mirror view. The producers of mass entertainments, themselves the products of this culture, both reflect, adapt, and alter standard images and values. Movie depictions of women may be fantasy projections, cruel distortions, or so-called realistic portrayals. Often, women are portrayed ideally; Linda Evans as Krystal Carrington on television's "Dynasty" is the ideal American beauty: blonde, statuesque, and angelic. The ideal bad woman counterpart, Alexis, played by Joan Collins, is a brunette, shorter in stature, and diabolical. Real life rarely offers such perfect contrasts.

While female pilots, reporters, and doctors were not common in the United States in the 1930s and 1940s, they appeared regularly on the movie screen. Audiences seemed to enjoy seeing women in atypical roles precisely because few of the above opportunities existed during the depression. In this sense, the cinematic portrayals were both ideal and fantasy images. They offered women's audiences heroic women to admire. Film historians have commented on the emergence of sinister women on the screens of the late 1940s and early 1950s. Suddenly, audiences were presented with murderous wives in great number. Did this describe reality or rather a director and writer's unconscious, psychological fear of the postwar world, a fear expressed as resentment toward women? Clearly, complex motives and processes are at work here.

The popularity of one image in one period over the others seems to say more about the times than the images. Marys had been popular during the early days of silent film, most notably in the careers of Mary Pickford and Lillian Gish, and in the 1950s in the movies of Debbie Reynolds and Doris Day, and on television, in the popular domestic comedies such as the "Dick Van Dyke Show" (Mary Tyler Moore) and the "Ozzie and Harriet Show" (Harriet Nelson). Both periods were postwar eras, times traditionally interested in reasserting old values, not experimenting with new ones. In the U.S. adaptation of the biblical Mary, and in one of our culture's most persistent paradoxes, Mary could be a wife and mother yet somehow, mysteriously, remain pure and asexual. She is the comforting symbol of family and traditional values in difficult times. Sexual women, in this dichotomous view, become Eves: immoral, disobedient, and dangerous. In popular culture, this makes them very desirable. While Eves are always with us, Marys become immensely appealing primarily in periods of turbulence and uncertainty.

Though one image may dominate a period, all three appear throughout popular cultural history. Moreover, in order to vary the images, Marys sometimes surprise audiences with their ability to take on independent qualities, while Eves can be reformed, and independent women succumb to the majoritarian values and give up their careers for romance and marriage. Independent woman-type Kathleen Turner, in the 1980s *Romancing the Stone* and *The Jewel of the Nile*, required a handsome, strong hero, Michael Douglas, to save her from disaster. The images interacted and strengthened each other. They endure because they possess real and authentic concerns: the wish to be sweet and cared for, the desire to express sexuality, and the need to be a unique individual. The three images, therefore, are expressed either archetypically or stereotypically in popular culture. The best examples remain true to the ideal archetype, while the more hackneyed portrayals fall into the category of stereotype.

Adventure, comedy, romance, melodrama, and horror, the popular conventions, include examples of all three images of women. Independent women appeared in adventure, romance, melodrama, and comedy, while Eve became a fixture in the western, the gangster, the romance, and the melodrama. Mary flourished in horror and science fiction films where she was being scared to death and then saved by the hero; in melodrama Mary suffered and was ultimately rewarded by the love of a good man. The independent woman might occasionally display her vulnerabilities, particularly in the romance and melodrama, where love overtook her wish for independence. For example, in her many movies of the 1930s and 1940s, Katharine Hepburn was always the strong individual but, especially in her films with Spencer Tracy, she often compromised her freedom at film's end for marital harmony.

The independent woman existed in nineteenth century fiction, but often in covert ways; in this century, she has existed on the burlesque stage and the movies. Hepburn, Bette Davis, Barbara Stanwyck, and many others portrayed the independent woman on screen in the 1930s and 1940s. And on television, Angie Dickinson, Lindsay Wagner, Tyne Daley, and Sharon Gless tracked criminals and displayed ingenuity in endeavors usually restricted to males. Indicative of the often paradoxical relationship of popular culture's offerings to reality, it was on television during the preliberated era, the 1960s, that women flourished, usually as comic independents, an interesting variation on the theme. Carol Burnett, Mary Tyler Moore, and Beatrice Arthur expressed their individuality, as long as it was done in a humorous mode. Transformation of form often cloaked the message. So independent women, even in the postliberation 1980s, usually are accompanied by trusty men in their adventurous pursuits.

Typecasting often characterized female performers. However, those who achieved stardom projected something of their own unique personality, charm, and power into their role. This was true of female singers, actresses, and television stars. Barbara Stanwyck was often identified as an Eve, but her spunk changed the image into that of an independent Eve. Mary Tyler Moore synthesized the Mary image with the independent woman on the "Mary Tyler Moore Show." She remained sweet and ladylike while speaking for women's rights. She expressed her commitment to equal opportunity while tremulously smiling at her boss, Mr. Grant.

The images portrayed in the popular media often blended with the personal biographies of the female stars. Throughout this century, audiences have read fan magazines to learn about their favorite stars; in their minds, the real-life experiences of the star and the fictional portrayals intermingled. Their biographies often confirmed the Horatio Alger expectations of the audience: poor girls made good in Hollywood. Thus, the real-life circumstances of the stars offered comfort and solace to those who wanted to continue believing in their own ability to achieve the American Dream of mobility and individual success. Though it is difficult to equate fan magazine renditions of a star's personal life with either the real life of the star or her screen roles, fans often blurred the lines between the three dimensions. During the heyday of the movies, fans read about Barbara Stanwyck's family troubles and of Carole Lombard's wisecracks. Greta Garbo's face appeared on many covers of *Modern Screen* and *Photoplay*, and Joan Crawford's fan clubs became the most numerous in the country. All of the major studios sent out glossy photographs of their stars to all requesters. Today, magazines as diverse as *People* and the *National Enquirer* supply fans with information on rock stars as well as television personalities.

To go into show business in the early twentieth century was an adventurous, unconventional route for a woman in this country. Being in the public eye, on display, required great confidence, acting ability, courage, and/or personal drive. Stars are atypical people, living lives unlike the majority. Women stars are even more unusual social types: economically independent, public women whose lives are seen by all. Fan magazines recognized their appeal and described the difficulties in reconciling career with marriage. Bette Davis, Carole Lombard, Joan Crawford, and many other Hollywood stars granted interviews on this subject. Once a performer achieved stardom, her public devoured all of the information it could get on her private life, her background, her likes, and her fears. In recent years, television interviewers quizzed female stars about their childhood, their dreams, and their sexual life. Soon the writer merged the star's private life with her public one; the performing roles interacted and blended with the private roles.

Often, stars are happy to explain themselves to their audiences. They want to bring order and coherence to their lives, to understand, along with their adoring followers, why they achieved fame, why they are admired. So they grant interviews and summarize their pasts. They present a logical, linear view of their lives to suggest prescience on their part (as Marilyn Monroe said, "I wanted to be a star since I was nine"). They unconsciously adopted the Horatio Alger model within which to relate their story. The star became the heroine in her private drama, overcoming adversity, just as she did in her imaginative roles. She also became a role model to her audiences.

The biographies of female performers usually reveal the fighter quality of the woman, the underdog willing to go against the odds. A large number of these women came from divorced families; some had childhood accidents that required long periods of recuperation that forced otherwise active young women to contemplate themselves and their future quietly. Doris Day and Carole Lombard, both youthful victims of car accidents, had to give up their dreams of becoming dancers. Mary Pickford, Fanny Brice, Marilyn Monroe, Bette Davis, and Doris Day all had divorced parents. Though their talents were each quite different from the other, they all showed perseverance and drive.

Enduring Values sets out to demonstrate the continuity and vitality of the dominant images of women in popular culture. Because popular culture reflects the larger cultural value system of the United States, it is eminently reasonable to assume that its views are compatible with mainstream attitudes and beliefs. Further, the profit motive governing popular entertainment necessitates noncontroversial presentations; this is especially true on television, the most significant mass entertainment ever. Finally, the predominantly male producers and female performers in show business have generally shared the culture's views of women. It is only in the late twentieth century, with the increase in women's education, effective birth control, and feminism that some actresses and singers display public interest in women's political, economic, and social issues. Prior to the last two decades, with notable exceptions (such as Katharine Hepburn), most movie stars, burlesque queens, and popular singers performed and left reforming to others.

Though there are problems with the stereotypical treatments of the Mary, Eve, and independent woman images, there are also strengths in the exciting portrayals of these images. When the combinations and the presentations are successful, the comic Eve, the independent Mary, and the independent woman offer audiences interesting portraits of women. When the most popular stars capture and perfect one image, or regular variations within an image, audiences reward them with their attendance at each and every performance.

The continuities between the generations, the enduring images of the great women comics, singers, and actresses, serve as an important link in our popular cultural forms. The heroines we admired and still admire remind us of our values, our fears, and our needs. Our support for Bette Midler and Carol Burnett, two entertaining and successful comics, spark some familiar human instinct for the idiosyncratic, the rebellious, and the exaggerated. Both starred in interesting, changing times, and both behaved in atypical ways. Each generation has witnessed vulnerable beauties destroyed by love, adventurous women invulnerable to loss, and funny women who saw humor in themselves and in everyone around them. The women stars of every era have satisfied basic human dreams.

Indeed, there are fundamental reasons why women, the anchors of the culture, are portrayed in enduring ways, generation after generation. The love of excitement and adventure, for women as well as men, requires portrayals of independent women. The need to be reassured of woman's central role as wife and mother demands popular cultural depictions of Marys. And Western culture's ambivalent and tortured view of female sexuality creates many Eves in popular culture. The following pages will explore the images, the performers, and the popular formulas.

1

Trapped by Love

It was in the egalitarian United States that love was available for all to experience. Arranged marriages, even among the very rich, were never popular in this country. De Tocqueville, who visited these shores in the 1830s, marveled at the freedom of young women. They chose their mates, and their choice was often based upon love, not parental and economic considerations. They displayed independence while conforming to society's expectations of them. Prior to the 1960s, the widely held assumption was that love led inevitably to marriage, marriages were made in heaven, and they lasted forever. Upon these views was based a romantic vision: the hero and heroine were both impossibly gorgeous, they knew immediately of their eternal attraction and devotion to each other, and they declared their undying love in rapturous tones.

While Jefferson's Declaration of Independence granted every citizen the right to pursue happiness, love and romance guaranteed it. Since the woman in this scenario needed love to be within the bounds of marriage in order to secure her adult destiny, she invested a great deal in the fantasy, the hopes, and the dreams of romance. She both loved and feared the pursuit, the tension, and the excitement that accompanied the game of love. After all, her life literally depended upon it. Though all this has changed in the sexually liberated world of today, the assumptions just described prevailed for a very long time. They insured women's devotion to romantic fiction, movies, and songs.

The human need for love, companionship, sex, and children insures the continual interest in the subject of romance. Within popular culture, there is no formula that cannot include a romantic interest. Be it a western, a science fiction story, or a gangster film, romance can play a role. Because of its prime importance to everyone, there is also a whole genre called romance that operates in popular literature, the movies, and less so on television. Often on television, romance joins with its close companion, melodrama. In this context, melodrama is the stuff of life; it is the story of family troubles, domestic strife, and social breakdowns. While romance is an essential part of life, it is often subsumed in melodrama. Juvenile delinquency, drug addiction, sexual impotency, and financial troubles take precedence over romance in daily living. Indeed, melodrama is what happens after romance results in marriage. Throughout our popular culture, romance in its pure form and romance in melodrama have been extremely successful types of women's entertainment.

Romance and beauty became tied together in poetry and in the imagination. The beauty was always female beauty. Her physical features, her ethereality, and her fragility were all united into romantic thinking. She was the beautiful creature to be won by the worthy hero. Within her was the unspoken sexuality that gave her the qualities of Eve, yet her sweetness and vulnerability insured a Mary image. The hero sought a Mary to protect and possess. He may also have wished for an Eve, whom he separated from his Mary. Eve promised infinite pleasure and no commitment, while Mary became the respectable wife and mother. One of the results of the sexual liberation of the post–1960s years is an openness in discussions of female sexuality. Women's romantic fantasies, in modern romance novels, movies, and television melodramas, also contain sexual fantasies.

In the classic, preliberation period, U.S. women read romances, written by both men and women, that confirmed traditional attitudes about love. The male initiated the romantic encounter, and the ending was always happy, which is to say, the couple got married. Then the melodrama of life began, also chronicled in countless fictions. During the 1930s, a whole group of movies, termed the "women's films" or the "weepies," developed in which the trials and tribulations of women were featured. Barbara Stanwyck, as the working-class mother in *Stella Dallas* (1936), brought tears to the eyes of women in the audience when she stood in the rain while watching her daughter marry a wealthy socialite. *New York Times* critic Frank Nugent said of Bette Davis's melodramatic performance in *Dark Victory*, "The mascara was running freely at the Music Hall yesterday."[1]

Writer Olga Martin, in describing the 1934 Motion Picture Production Code, captured the nation's commitment to happy endings in their romances: "The American audience in particular demands a 'cheerful ending' in answer to a deeply-felt human need for a kindly philosophy of life."[2] In melodramas, however, the very opposite view prevailed. Daily life, filled with domestic travails, rarely ended, let alone ended happily. Thus, movie and television melodramas proliferated. But romance was often an important feature in melodramas; love sought, gained, and lost provided a dramatic center for most of them.

Pursuing both romance and independence seems incompatible. Yet women's search for both has often provided the very tension and excitement that powered the film or television program. The desire of the audience for the heroine to achieve both gives excitement to the story. Further, in the ideal world, the fantasy world of the viewer, the heroine accomplishes both; she gains love while retaining her individuality. Greta Garbo's many films in which her beauty led her to lovers who tried to subdue her became emblematic of the type. Similarly, the career woman, in most of the films of the 1930s, sought love as well as professional satisfaction; otherwise, she ran the risk of being described as "beautiful brain, beautiful clothes, no temperature, no pulse," the description applied to Rosalind Russell in the 1942 *Take a Letter, Darling*. The very successful advertising executive was not humanized until she fell in love.

Love and romance often win out in the struggle, since independent women, along with the Marys and Eves, cannot escape from the need, temptation, and snare of romance. Indeed, throughout the history of U.S. popular culture, whether we look at literature, burlesque, vaudeville, silent and sound film, television, or popular music, we find numerous examples of romantic heroines, women determined by the love in their lives. Female movie stars have played out their careers as love-lost or love-found heroines. Greta Garbo's agonized facial expression, presumably caused by the latest love of her life, became her trademark as well as the shorthand sign of a romance gone wrong. Audiences have given their love and loyalty to romantic heroines in all of the popular cultural forms. Since Susannah Rowson wrote her popular novel in the 1790s about a seduced and abandoned woman, novelists, lyricists, movie scenarists, and television script writers have flourished by writing about women in love, women falling out of love, women pursuing and being pursued, women sacrificing for love, and women generally being determined by love. When romantic love fails as a captivating theme, mother love enters. Though such productions as *Dark Victory* and "Edge of Night" outnumber films like *Stella Dallas*, the latter also have a place in the love lexicon of popular culture.

In the popular mind, certain movie stars have become closely identified with the romantic image. Their careers have been encaptured in the love tradition. Though they may have made other kinds of films, they became symbols of romance to their fans. Greta Garbo, for example, played a career woman in some of her films, but the dominant image she projected was of a romantic heroine, a woman determined by the love in her life. Elizabeth

Taylor also became the romantic heroine to the 1950s generation of moviegoers. Of all the popular cultural media, it was in the movies that the romantic heroine flourished. And it was through the persona of favorite women movie stars that romance was played out. By contrast, daytime television melodramas, and recent nighttime ones, contain romantic elements, but they are not the all-consuming focus as they were in romantic movies.

Movies in the United States portrayed pure, respectable love as well as its exciting, illicit counterpart. In silent film, Lillian Gish played innocent and virginal child-women who relied upon men to be their protectors.[3] At the same time, an important part of the attraction of Gish on the screen was her inner strength, her stamina under pressure, and her essential dignity. In 1912 she joined director D. W. Griffith to star in some of his greatest movies: *Birth of a Nation* (1915), *Intolerance* (1916), *Broken Blossoms* (1919), *Way Down East* (1920), and *Orphans of the Storm* (1921).

Always referring to her as "Miss Lillian," Griffith featured the angelic, fragile beauty of Gish. She personified his view of the good woman: sweet and dependent on men, yet strong in adversity. Griffith photographed Gish with an arc of light, suggesting a halo, around her face and head. Her delicate sweetness, physical slightness, and vulnerable pose made her the perfect Griffith heroine. As Elsie Stoneman in his monumental *Birth of a Nation*, Gish portrayed the southern belle who withstood many difficulties and ended happily with the hero. In *Way Down East*, Gish played a poor and innocent young woman named Anna who was tricked into a mock marriage with a wealthy scoundrel. Abandoned while pregnant, she had the child in a strange town, lost the child, and became a domestic worker to survive. Though she fell in love with the employer's son, she discouraged his attentions as she could "never marry anyone." After an unlikely set of circumstances, Anna, lost in a snowstorm, awakened on an ice float rushing toward a waterfall. The heroic employer's son saved her, of course, at the last moment; her past life was forgiven and everything ended happily.

During the 1920s, Gish starred in other silent films, most notably *La Boheme* (1926) and *The Scarlet Letter* (1926). Gish's trademark, of an inherently virtuous woman subjected to society's abuse, won her the sympathy of the audience in each and every portrayal. Thus, even in an uncharacteristic role of a disreputable woman, Gish sustained her demeanor of goodness and purity. In contrast to the innocence of Gish's screen character, Greta Garbo personified illicit love on the screen, the Eve who loved outside the boundaries of respectable society. Therefore, she was usually punished at the conclusion of the movie.

Women, as the chief agents of the culture, and as potential mothers, bore the responsibility for containing romance within marriage. But while the rules of society were always upheld, audiences sympathized with the sufferings of the illicit Garbo heroine. Her hurts and her frustrations won supporters in the audience. Garbo's greatest movies, both silent and sound, revolved around love themes. *Love* (1927) was an early version of the Anna Karenina story, which she remade in 1935 as *Anna Karenina*. In *Queen Christina* (1933) Garbo played the historical queen of Sweden, an able ruler who gave up her throne for the man she loved. At one point in the movie, she said, "It had been so enchanting to be a woman, not a queen, but a woman in a man's arms."[4] Her earlier displays of leadership qualities disappeared once she fell in love. It became the determining, and the destroying, factor in her life. In *Camille* she was the tubercular courtesan who claimed to live life frivolously and without ties; but when she too fell in love and later abandoned her lover for his own good, she could never recapture her former joy of living. Death claimed her, as it did in all of her other romances, with the exception of *Queen Christina*. Illicit romance, in Hollywood's scheme of values, had to end unhappily for the heroine, though the hero often remained unscathed.

A sense of determinism pervaded the atmosphere of all the films of that era. The beautiful woman had no choice; her life was determined by her lover; she was not free to go on living after the affair ended. Her options were severely limited. Ironically, beauty, a much desired and sought after commodity in women, did not insure eternal happiness, but the very opposite.

Bette Davis built a career on aspects of romance. She began by playing the gangster's loyal girlfriend and graduated to two variations on the theme: as the independent Eve and as the woman victimized by, and dependent upon, love. She played a woman who killed the husband she no longer loved in *Bordertown* (1935); the career woman who resisted marriage in *Ex-Lady* (1933); the call girl who remained loyal to her working colleagues in *Marked Woman* (1937); the rich, spoiled woman who learned humility through love (and death) in *Dark Victory* (1939); and the ugly duckling who was transformed by love in *Now, Voyager* (1942). Given Davis's long and prolific career, these are only a few of her portrayals of women in love.[5]

Bette Davis is usually viewed as one of the few independent women stars in Hollywood who created a persona of uniqueness, of difference from the stereotype. Yet, in her screen roles, she was largely confined to the romantic theme. The overwhelming commitment in U.S. culture to love and marriage for women makes it extremely difficult for even the strongest personalities to escape the mold. Katharine Hepburn and Rosalind Russell shared with Davis the position of able actress with a strong sense of individuality. But they too found that the man in their life decided their ultimate fate. For Hepburn it was either Spencer Tracy or Cary Grant; for Russell it was Fred MacMurray and for Davis, George Brent. In all cases, they gave up their careers for the men they loved; whether as journalists (Hepburn in *Woman of the Year*; Davis in *Front Page Woman*, Russell in *His Girl Friday*) or as business executives (Russell in *Take a Letter, Darling* and Hepburn in

Desk Set), they found romance the overriding consideration of their lives, a subject to be explored in greater depth in Chapter 3.

Elizabeth Taylor was to the filmgoers of the 1950s what Garbo had been to an earlier generation. She was the romantic queen, the beautiful actress whose life on an off the screen interested her fans. She was photographed constantly for newspapers and magazines, as was Garbo earlier. Her stunning beauty decided her screen fate. She often became the temptress, the illicit love who used her gorgeousness to attract, seduce, and control the male, but for this, she was always punished. While she was respectable love in *Giant* (1956), she was the passionate wife (though treated as a whore by her husband) in *Cat on a Hot Tin Roof* (1958), the mistress in *Butterfield Eight* (1960), the conniving queen *Cleopatra* (1963), and the shrew in *Who's Afraid of Virginia Woolf?* (1966) and the *Taming of the Shrew* (1967). Because male writers and directors have always found illicit love more exciting and cinematically worthy than conventionally married love, and because they have usually viewed the beautiful woman as suspect, they portrayed Taylor as both desired and punished, lovely and repulsive. Elizabeth Taylor's screen career has been shaped by these attitudes, and though she has willingly chosen roles that showed her in an unattractive light, the bulk of her portrayals have been within the illicit love genre.[6]

Marshall McLuhan's definition of television as a cool medium, in contrast to the heat of the movies, may partially explain the absence of romantic heroines on television. After all, in the well-lit room in which television is viewed, often with other people around, and with conversation and commercials breaking one's concentration, it is difficult to sustain the intensity of a romantic narrative. But perhaps there is another underlying, unspoken cultural reality that prevents romance from being featured on television today: romance is more difficult to achieve in a sexually liberated era. Easy and casual sexual encounters have replaced singular, formal romantic meetings. Romance has been stripped of its mystery by its reduction to sex. Direct, informal conversations between the sexes have replaced formal introductions, engineered after much planning and plotting. Women can choose their sexual partners, a practice never allowed before. Love affairs break up regularly on television melodramas, but the excitement of the chase, the pursuit of romance, is largely over, a victim of changed times.

No one pays for his or her sins in the guilt-free United States of the 1980s. Anna Karenina would not be punished for abandoning her son for her lover. She would not be shunned by society's best. There are few risks or consequences in a sexually permissive society. Indeed, the real social concerns, now portrayed on television melodramas, are the fear of AIDS or herpes, not the fear of losing one's virginity. Human misunderstandings and missed opportunities still thwart romance, as they always did in the past, but good communication is the goal of the period, and all women are encouraged to express themselves freely, with no more inhibitions and no more censorship. The tensions and problems of everyday life as well as the pressure to succeed in the business and professional worlds have overtaken the young; there is little time for luxury of romance. The pursuit has to be condensed and consummation quickly achieved.

John Cawelti, in a study of the romantic formula published over a decade ago, assumed that the women's liberation movement would create new romantic conventions. New women, in a new age, would abandon the old formulas and invent new ones more suitable to the new values and behavior of life in the 1980s. But he also anticipated another possibility, that it would "lead to a total rejection of the moral fantasy of love triumphant."[7] Cawelti assumed that liberated women would reject the fantasy of true love as fraudulent. Independent women would no longer subscribe to a fantasy that expected them to surrender themselves to love.

Actually, neither alternative came to pass. Women did not create new feminist romances, nor did they abandon the traditional romances. For the most part, the few movies and made-for-TV-movies that contain romantic elements operate within the traditional genre and women's audiences appear to accept that. The heroine may be a career woman, but love is still central to her life. Just as Rosalind Russell, in the 1942 *Take a Letter, Darling* gave up her career for love, so Meryl Streep in the 1986 *Heartburn* could not concentrate on her writing because of love problems.

The coolness of television has been more conducive to the sweet Mary image of woman, the good woman for whom romance led to respectable marriage, children, and eternal happiness. In the many family series of the 1950s and early 1960s, good wives dominated. From "The Aldrich Family" and "Father Knows Best" to "Ozzie and Harriet" and the "Dick Van Dyke Show," television viewers were presented with obedient wives.[8] Laurie Petrie, played by the still unliberated Mary Tyler Moore, accepted her role gladly, and while Harriet Nelson sometimes quipped about her expected behavior, she too seemed pleased with her life.

By the mid–1960s, this type disappeared from television to be replaced late in the decade by more assertive women, new representatives of the independent woman mode. But while television was young, tame romance, in the form of the happy housewife, suggested that women were not trapped by love, but actively sought it and enjoyed married, conventional love above all choices. Because romance was presented in its Mary-like guise, within the confines of marriage, it was treated as comedy, not tragedy. Married love lent itself to comedy, while illicit love had the potential for intensity and tragic ends.

On 1980s television, primarily in the melodramas, lovers are seen in bed together. Because the mode is melodrama, and not romance, the love relationship is consummated early and the subsequent trials and tribulations deal with children, unfaithfulness, financial problems, and a myriad of other social and personal difficulties. Traditional romantic themes like unfulfilled love, thwarted love, and misunderstandings are largely absent from melodrama. Rather, the misunderstandings arise after sexual fulfillment and are based on other factors.

In sexually liberated times, where nothing is forbidden, nothing is withheld. Mystery, delay, and denial, common romantic elements, no longer exist in the love relationships of the 1980s. Love and sex have been separated from each other in new ways: in traditional times, when a double standard prevailed, men distinguished between good women, whom they married, and bad women with whom they had sexual encounters. Women were taught that love and marriage, if one were respectable, were always tied together. Today, sexual experience is easily available to both sexes; so women can behave as men have.

But the wish for enduring relationships persists; in the new lexicon, love is translated into commitment, but relationships do not necessarily result in marriage. Marriages are no longer made in heaven, nor do they last forever. Undying love, true love, loses its meaning in this age of possibility. Romance, in popular culture and in real life, flounders and disappears. It is replaced with the constant strife of television melodrama. The denial and delay of sexual fulfillment no longer exist. They cannot when there is no long period of anticipation, of unfulfilled expectation, of fantasy, and of dreaming, all essential ingredients of romance. So love and romance become enveloped in family quarrels, financial troubles, and social anxieties. The path, after easy sexual encounters and without romance, becomes a melodramatic obstacle course.

NOTES

1. Frank S. Nugent, "Dark Victory," *New York Times*, April 21, 1939, p. 27.
2. Olga J. Martin, *Hollywood's Movie Commandments* (New York: H. W. Wilson, 1937), p. 53.
3. Sources on Gish's life and career include Lillian Gish with Ann Pinchot, *Lillian Gish: The Movies, Mr. Griffith and Me* (Englewood Cliffs, N.J.: Prentice Hall, 1969) and Romano Tozzi, "Lillian Gish," *Films in Review* 13 (December 1962) pp. 580–585.
4. *Queen Christina*, MGM, 1933.
5. Bette Davis, *The Lonely Life* (New York: G. P. Putnam, 1962).
6. Dick Sheppard, *Elizabeth Taylor* (New York: Warner Books, 1975).
7. John Cawelti, *Adventure, Mystery, and Romance: Formula Stories as Art and Popular Culture* (Chicago: University of Chicago Press, 1976), p. 42.
8. See Diana M. Meehan, *Ladies of the Evening: Women Characters of Prime-Time Television* (Metuchen, N.J.: Scarecrow Press, 1983), esp. chap. 4.

2

Covert and Overt Resisters: Women Writers as Challengers

The writing of novels has always been within the province of women's activities. Historically, in fact, many of the most popular novelists in the United States have been women. The successful women writers, however, faced a unique dilemma, a knotty struggle unknown to their male counterparts. They had to sacrifice their particular visions to conform to cultural expectations about women. This problem was more true in past centuries; one consequence of the more liberated decades of the late twentieth century is that popular women writers express sexual longings, describe unconventional heroines, and produce ambiguous endings in their work.

Nineteenth century women scribes had to satisfy their female readers (and most novel readers to this day remain women), who had a definite set of cultural expectations for their fictional fare. Atypical characters, immoral heroines, or defiant women were unwelcome in fiction; female readers boycotted daring authors. Thus, writers who strove for rich complexity and variety in their portrayals always ran the risk of creating types that were too unusual and would be unappealing to their audiences. Women creators of fiction were not expected to be artists, but rather popular merchants satisfying their growing readership.

Prior to the twentieth century, the artistic dilemma was resolved by not facing it; women became popular writers precisely because they catered to the tastes and values of their audience. They upheld virtue, virginity, and community values and did not challenge the status quo. When their heroines behaved in socially disapproved ways, they always paid for their indiscretion; if a man compromised their virtue, they paid with their life or sometimes less severely with the loss of social support and the taking away of their illegitimate offspring. One sexual indiscretion led to pregnancy, and it was the woman, not the man, who suffered. All fictional heroines were expected to be sweet Marys, patient and obedient, waiting for Mr. Right to wisk them away into holy matrimony.

Upholders of cultural values such as Mrs. E. D. E. N. Southworth and Harriet Beecher Stowe found approval from their faithful audiences.[1] Susannah Rowson, the writer in 1791 of the first U.S. bestseller, *Charlotte Temple, A Tale of Truth*, explicitly stated in her preface that she wrote the book "For the perusal of the young and thoughtless of the fair sex."[2] The story described the evil end that came to an innocent 15-year-old girl who allowed her love for a handsome soldier to lead her astray. Seduced and abandoned, Charlotte died after giving birth to a baby. It was Charlotte who was responsible, not the soldier; though she was portrayed as an innocent victim, she paid the consequence for her sexual indiscretion. Women who wrote endless tales based upon this very same theme found scores of readers; women devoured each melodramatic tale and each reenforcement of cultural imperatives. Women must be chaste before marriage, obedient first to their fathers and then to their husbands, and become the moral upholders of the family. Popular fiction, primarily written by women, confirmed this message.

While most nineteenth century female writers defended the moral precepts of the culture and indeed were active confirmers of its values, a few became covert resisters, clever questioners of the roles and life goals assigned to women. To remain acceptable to their readers, they expressed their resistance to dominant attitudes about women in involuted ways. They could not openly declare their contempt or direct a frontal attack upon social norms; their resistance had to be covert. Sometimes they walked a delicate tightrope, first suggesting atypical female behavior and then returning to traditional expectations. At other times, they voiced their dissent in mock and humorous ways so as not to offend their readers. When, on the rare occasions, their resistance became open, they lost their audience.

The writers of the last century included in this discussion set the stage for the twentieth century's images, in literature and in the electronic media, of independent women types. Their spunky literary creations provided the foundation for this century's depictions of unique women in the movies and on television. Harriet Prescott Spofford (1835–1921), for example, a well-regarded popular novelist whose writing career spanned more than 50 years but who is forgotten to twentieth century readers, operated within the first model suggested: her female characters often experienced unusual events and behaved in atypical ways, only to embrace traditional patterns at the end. Mary Wilkins Freeman (1852–1930) created heroines who coped with the life dictated for them in stoical, often self-confident ways. Freeman's heroines mocked male foibles, a good but subtle form of covert resistance, and displayed female strength. Kate Chopin (1851–1904), perhaps the ablest of all nineteenth century women writers, had heroines who expressed their displeasure in more and more explicit ways—as a result, editors refused to publish her stories.

The preponderance of restless female protagonists in the fiction of these three writers suggests one respectable means to challenge the dominant patterns of the culture. Few heroines in fiction openly defied conventions; few resisted marriage, and few set out for the territories; indeed, few did so in real life either. But the fact of restlessness demonstrated unhappiness. Some of them went a step further and developed ingenious ways of expressing their displeasure with social expectations of female behavior. Some sublimated and channeled their discontent into socially useful directions. With the benefit of modern psychology, we know that humans can be adaptive and imaginative in coping with frustration. Fictional heroines showed themselves to be flexible and creative in their forms of resistance.

Harriet Prescott Spofford wrote hundreds of stories and many novels during her literary career. Her stories cannot be conveniently labeled under one genre, nor were all her female characters covert resisters of the culture's values.[3] But some of her best remembered works portrayed powerful women who stepped outside predictable social behavior. In "Circumstance," a young woman was caught by an Indian devil in the forest while returning home from attending a sick person.[4] She kept him at bay by singing to him. Though her voice grew weaker, she continued to sing through the night until her husband heard her and saved her. The story possessed a strange power and evoked an admirable feeling for the courageous heroine. Though the ending was traditional, the ingenuity, strength, and courage of the young woman gave the story its excitement.

In many of Spofford's stories, heroines were artists, creative spirits whose art dominated their lives. In "Desert Sands," both Mr. Sydney and his wife, Eos, were artists; he would not allow her to paint, instead insisting that she live for him alone. After a grueling trip to Africa that weakened Eos, she grew steadily sicker and eventually died. Sydney was portrayed as selfish and utterly ruthless. He had taken away the creative expression of his wife and thus snuffed out her life. Sydney declared: "I did not love Art well enough to give my wife to it; I did not want a rival in her; above all, I could not have her sacred name on everybody's lips. She was mine, not theirs."

In this story, the wife withered away under the smothering treatment of her husband; she did not assert herself before him, but caved in. He acknowledged his power over her when he said: "I loved her only as a part of myself. I allowed her no integral life."[5] Spofford's message was clear: a woman artist needed her work as much as a man did, and wifely devotion should be secondary to artistic expression. "I allowed her no integral life" was Sydney's final judgment on his wife's death. This became the author's moving critique of a man's treatment of a woman. Spofford's moral anger was evident.

Spofford's women came from many different classes and exhibited a wide variety of personalities. Some of her women were self-possessed, such as Delphine in "In A Cellar"; her beauty helped her to achieve her life's ambition. Delphine admitted to an admirer: "We all build our own houses and then complain that they cramp us here. . . . while the fault is not in the other, but in us, who increase here and shrink there without reason."[6] Another self-aware heroine named Louisa, who enjoyed using her natural beauty to manipulate men for her own amusement (another form of coping), acknowledged that she would not marry an ardent admirer because he was poor: "He can't afford to marry. I can't afford to marry—with a difference. He will go on with his pictures that never sell. I shall go on with my flirtations that always sell."[7]

Many of the female characters depicted by Spofford resisted values imposed upon them; rather, they reshaped the values to their own benefit. The beautiful women in Spofford's stories used their beauty to make good marriages. By contrast, Ruth Yetton in *Azarian: An Episode* (1864), earned a living by sketching, but then she fell in love, in true romantic fashion, with an artist named Azarian, who used her and then left her.[8] Her life lost all meaning and she contemplated suicide. To this point in the story, Spofford had written a rather typical romantic melodrama. Ruth wondered what her life meant: "Who values it? Nobody. Nobody in the wide world. Why should she keep it?"[9] But then she heard a helmsman sing, and she became, somewhat mysteriously, transformed: "for an instant her personal misery lifted over a quick flash of gratitude for the perfect loveliness of the world."[10] Ruth resolved to make a life for herself again, and with the help of a woman friend, she began to renew herself. She adopted two orphan boys and returned to drawing. The narrator mused:

Is it, when all is said, the lover or the love that one requires? Think of Goethe, and say the love. Think of any woman, and answer that it is the pulsating personality of the lover. But falling torn and bleeding, the arms of a true and strong affection, be it whose it may, can support one 'til health of the heart returns.[11]

It was a woman's friendship that restored Ruth to good health, and now "heart free and hand free in the service of unselfish love, Ruth soared on her art with wings she had not found before. She lived the life she coveted, she had her work, she had her bliss, these were her children."[12] The imagery of flight and freedom, of one's own inspired work, was not generally associated with the lives of women. Spofford suggested the unconventional notion that useful and creative work, combined with child rearing, offered women opportunities for worthiness. The love of a man was not essential to their happiness.

Azarian was a good example of Spofford's delicate balancing of traditional sentiments with searching heroines. Ruth's artistic talent and her refusal to die for her lover put her in a category above the typical heroine who died willingly for lost love. Useful work, female friendship, and children were still viewed as the most significant human endeavors. Yet Spofford did not reject the love of a man as a woman's destiny; she simply and pragmatically advised her readers that a scorned woman could live happily and constructively. Spofford gave her readers heroines who not only endured but created self-definitions, without men and traditional families. She offered a fictional world of independent women.

Spofford's heroine in "Jo and I" overcame her deep-seated fear of storms to venture forth and rescue her husband and another man lost in the snow.[13] In "Mrs. Hetty's Husband," Hetty Duneagle was selfish and destructive. She so aggravated her husband that he was driven away only to be killed. Mrs. Hetty then mourned him as a dutiful widow.[14] She was a destructive form of covert resister who turned her hostility and personal discontent against the social authority figure in her life, her husband. Indeed, many heroines who sacrificed their own happiness and, sometimes, their own lives for others represented another form of covert resistance. Within the corpus of Harriet Prescott Spofford's work, one can find all kinds of women: the traditional self-sacrificer, the stoic, the bold, and the destructive. The diversity of her heroines offered instructive insights into many ways women coped with their place in life.

Mary Wilkins Freeman was also a prolific and popular writer of the second half of the nineteenth century. She published 15 novels and 18 collections of short stories. Like Spofford, the short story was her métier. While Spofford's women traveled around and often lived in big cities, Freeman's heroines lived in the cold farmlands of New England. In her most famous story, "A New England Nun," the heroine Louisa waited 15 years for her betrothed to return from Australia.

She had been faithful to him all these years. She had never dreamed of the possibility of marrying anyone else. Her life, especially for the last seven years, had been full of pleasant peace; she had never felt discontented nor impatient over her lover's absence; still, she had always looked forward to his return and their marriage as the inevitable conclusion of things. However, she had fallen into a way of placing it so far in the future that it was almost equal to placing it over the boundaries of another life.[15]

When Louisa learned that her returned fiancé loved another woman, she broke the engagement, not telling him the reason why. "If Louisa Ellis had sold her birthright she did not know it, the taste of the pottage was so delicious, and had been her sole satisfaction for so long. Serenity and placid narrowness had become to her as the birthright itself."[16]

Louisa exemplified a covert resister. Though dutifully conventional on the surface, she found in her fiancé's absence a pleasant existence that she chose to continue. As Freeman concluded: "Serenity and placid narrowness had become to her as the birthright itself." The readers of "A New England Nun" may have pitied the spinster Louisa, but some may have wondered whether she had not chosen an alternative lifestyle that also had its attractions. Surely Freeman's Louisa was pleased with the arrangement.

In another story, "The Revolt of Mother," a farmer's wife, who had loyally worked with her husband for 40 years and had raised two children, wanted a nicer farmhouse. But her stubborn husband ignored her wishes and kept building new barns and expanding the farm. While he was away, the wife moved the family into the newest barn; upon his return, the farmer relented and agreed to convert the barn into a house.[17] In "A Humble Romance," Sally, a poor orphan girl, married an itinerant tin salesman after a few moments' acquaintance. Their marriage was happy until one day he told her he had to go away after extracting her promise to bear up under any circumstance. She did and three years later he returned. They resumed their marriage after he explained that he left to earn money.[18] In both this story as well as "The Revolt of Mother," the women emerged as strong, uncomplaining people whose virtues were tested by extremely difficult husbands.

The women portrayed by Mary Wilkins Freeman always endured and often prevailed. They resisted male authority either overtly as in "The Revolt of Mother" or covertly as in "A New England Nun." In "Old Woman Magoun," grandmother Magoun raised her granddaughter Lily by herself and protected the girl from all outside influences. At 14, Lily was lovely but childlike. Mrs. Magoun, a civic leader, got the townsmen to build a much needed bridge. "It seems queer to me," she said, "that men can't do nothin' without havin' to drink and chew to keep their sperits up. Lord! I've worked all my life and never done nuther." Her friend Sally Jinks responded, "Men is different." Old Woman Magoun had the last word: "Yes, they be," which she said "with open contempt."[19]

Tragedy befell Mrs. Magoun during the course of the story, perhaps because she uttered such critical words about men. Threatened with the possibility of losing her granddaughter to her carousing son-in-law (and after unsuccessfully trying to get Lily adopted by respectable folks in town), Mrs. Magoun allowed the girl to eat poisonous berries that resulted in her death. Freeman had established the old woman's character early in the story: "But Old Woman Magoun had within her a mighty sense of reliance upon herself as being on the right track in the midst of a maze of evil, which gave her courage."[20] Rather than allow her granddaughter to be corrupted by her father and his drinking friends, she sacrificed her young life, a difficult, dramatic, and controversial decision.

"Old Woman Magoun" was yet another example of bold resistance to social norms though done in covert and unusual ways. "The Gospel According to Joan" offered another view of Freeman's tendency to mock society. A young girl named Joan boldly stole a woman's needlework and resold it to her in order to feed some orphans in town. None of the townspeople, though it was Christmastime, helped the needy; so Joan acted and stole for the benefit of the orphans. She defended her behavior upon being caught, and the minister of the town, somewhat awed by her audacity, concluded, "There she goes, little anarchist, holy-hearted in holy cause, and if her way be not as mine, who am I to judge?"[21]

This extraordinary conclusion placed this story beyond the boundaries of most conventional tales. Freeman seemed to be saying that unusual behavior, done in the service of absolute morality, must be forgiven. Perhaps there are human needs that transcend social barriers and require new forms of acting. The heroines of Mary Wilkins Freeman offered her readers a great deal to think about. Louisa, the farmer's wife, old woman Magoun, and Joan presented readers with unusual examples of covert resistance to cultural norms.

Kate Chopin qualified as the boldest challenger of the culture's view of women in the late nineteenth century. While she had a reputation as a local colorist whose short stories about Creoles and Cajun society were well regarded, it was in her women's stories that Kate Chopin broke new ground.[22] Her fiction dealt openly with the sensuous needs and unspoken passion of women, a subject never discussed publicly in Catholic New Orleans or Puritan New England. Her contemporaries did not admit to the fact that women had sexual natures, and they surely did not read fiction that described female passion.

Thus, Kate Chopin attacked social norms head-on. She believed that the emotional life of women was their most important resource and that her interior explorations of self provided a rich area for fiction. At the same time, she portrayed women who sought social roles for themselves as well as those who performed good deeds for those less able. All of Chopin's women appeared, however, as restless, questing people, unhappy with society's definition of them. Chopin questioned marriage, wifehood, and motherhood, the essential trilogy for women.

In "The Story of an Hour," one of the most powerful three-page stories ever written, Mrs. Mallard, a young, frail wife, learned that her husband had been killed in a railroad accident. After retiring to her room, her grief was followed by a sense of liberation: "There would be no one to live for during those coming years; she would live for herself. There would be no powerful will bending her in that blind persistence with which men and women believe they have a right to impose a private will upon a fellow-creature."[23] Mrs. Mallard's sudden widowhood produced a surge of new energy and hope for a self-fulfilled life, one in which she could satisfy her own desires. But her blissful moment was interrupted with the discovery that her husband was not on the train. As he appeared in the hallway, she fainted and died, her death called heart failure. This story flew in the face of conventional literature. A widow felt joy on her personal liberation; she expressed these feelings to herself without a sense of guilt or revulsion, and she stopped living when this new hope died.

It was not uncommon for readers to be startled by Chopin's stories. In "Fedora," a 30-year-old woman acted as hostess at her family home. She was an emotionally closed woman who could not express her love for Malthers, a family friend. The dramatic incident occurs when Fedora volunteers to pick up Malthers's sister at the station. Fedora told the young woman:

"You know, dear child . . . I want you to feel completely at home with us. . . . I feel that I shall be quite fond of you." When the girl looked up into her face, with murmured thanks, Fedora bent down and pressed a long, penetrating kiss upon her mouth.

Malthers' sister appeared astonished, and not too well pleased. Fedora, with seemingly unruffled composure, gathered the reins, and for the rest of the way stared steadily ahead of her between the horses' ears.[24]

Chopin's women came from all classes, though aristocratic women received most of her attention. In "Miss McEnders,"[25] she satirized an upper-class self-righteous woman who delivered speeches before the Woman's Reform Club but really had no idea about the working conditions of the poor. While preparing for her marriage to a rich middle-aged man, she discovered that her young seamstress was the mother of a child. Miss McEnders demanded to know why the woman pretended to be a mademoiselle, and the reply was: "Life is not all couleur de rose, Mees McEndairs; you do not know what life is, you!"[26] The protagonist later learned, to her great consternation, that both her father and her fiancé had earned their fortunes in dubious ways.

In a story never published during her lifetime, "The Storm," Chopin described a sexual encounter between a married woman and a former boyfriend while a storm brewed. The woman's husband and child were in town, leaving her alone on the family plantation.[27]

The generous abundance of her passion, without guile or trickery, was like a white flame which penetrated and found response in depths of his own sensuous nature that had never yet been reached. When he touched her breasts they gave themselves up in quivering ecstasy, inviting his lips. Her mouth was a fountain of delight. And when he possessed her, they seemed to swoon together at the very borderland of life's mystery.[28]

U.S. readers in the late Victorian era were not ready for this explicit description of sexual pleasure, pleasure shared equally by the woman. After the storm, the lover left, her family returned, and the family sat down to a happy dinner together. The lover wrote to his wife, who was visiting in Biloxi, and suggested that she stay another month if she were having a good time. His wife had the last word: "And the first free breath since her marriage seemed to restore the pleasant liberty of her maiden days. Devoted as she was to her husband, their intimate conjugal life was something which she was more than willing to forego for a while."[29]

So the storm passed and everyone was happy. It is evident why Kate Chopin did not publish this story in 1898; no one would have it. When her novella, *The Awakening*, was published the following year, it proved to be too much for the traditional reading public as well, and the reviews were so damning that Chopin stopped writing and in 1904, at the age of 53, she died.

The novella explored the sensual and intellectual awakening of Edna Pontellier, a New Orleans wife and mother married to a staid businessman. During a summer stay at a resort, Edna met and fell in love with a young man named Robert Lebrun. They became constant companions, and by the end of the summer, she began to "realize her position in the universe as a human being, and to recognize her relations as an individual to the world within and about her." Upon returning to the city, Edna began to paint and eventually moved out of her husband's home for a small one of her own. Though she loved her two sons and would give her life for her children, "I would not give myself," she commented.[30] She could not explain what she meant by this remark, but in her heart she understood.

According to Chopin, Edna "had resolved never again to belong to another than herself."[31] *The Awakening* described her restless and persistent search for a self and for self-satisfaction. She never found it. In the end, she walked into the ocean, never to return to shore. During the course of the novella, however, Edna tried painting, a love affair with another man, being the nice hostess, and ended up dissatisfied with all of these solutions. She was not a good artist and realized it; further, passionate love of a man other than her husband could not be tolerated in traditional society. No path seemed open to her, and so she committed suicide. Edna Pontellier's intense exploration of a lifestyle that suited her sounds extraordinarily relevant to modern readers. It shocked the audiences of 1899. Her hometown of St. Louis refused to put the book in its library, and the respectable *Nation* commented, "We cannot see that literature or the criticism of life is helped by the detailed history of the manifold and contemporary love affairs of a wife and mother."[32]

Kate Chopin's fiction discussed the inner and outer life of a woman. She explored the usually unspoken sexual feelings of a woman at the same time that she described women who rejected the wifely and motherly roles. Her women wanted to strip themselves of social definitions and to examine anew what their natures were. The unconventional subject matter, the frank discussions of female sexuality, and the absolute lack of guilt in her heroines all marked them for doom in the traditional United States. Women readers were simply not prepared for overt resistance to social norms; they could not exhibit anything but disgust and shock at stories that described widows rejoicing over their sudden emancipation or heroines who were unhappy with their status as upper-class women occupying a home with a considerate, well-providing husband. In the 1970 reprint of 20 of her stories and *The Awakening*, the heroines in 9 of the stories consciously rejected marriage.

The story lines and women characters of Kate Chopin were so different, so atypical, that they literally shocked her readers. Editors were startled with her sensuous descriptions of sexual experience; moralists were outraged by women kissing other women or seamstresses boldly having children out of wedlock and then criticizing their employers' conduct. Chopin questioned both the culture's definition of women as well as the conspiratorial silence over the emotional needs and experiences of women. She glorified the ecstasy of good sexual experiences and viewed intercourse between loving people as one important form of self-fulfillment as well as transcendence of self.

She wondered what the nature of woman was after her social roles were stripped away. Surely, Chopin believed, sexuality existed for women. But what were the other dimensions of women's personality? What were their other possible pleasures in life? Kate Chopin tried asking these questions in her fiction, but she found no readers for such an exploration. Her failure to win an audience is dramatic testimony to my claim that female writers had to operate within cultural norms, at least until recently, in order to be published and read. On the surface, Kate Chopin led a rather conventional life, but in her fiction, she opened up doors into rooms that most people wanted shut tightly.

Chopin ranks as the most daring of the female writers of the last century. Her prose faced forbidden subjects and portrayed women sympathetically as they rejected traditional behavior. While the women depicted by Mary Wilkins Freeman and Harriet Prescott Spofford sometimes showed spunk and ingenuity, they always remained within social boundaries. Neither their emotional lives nor their social roles were explored in detail, and though they sometimes acted independently of men, they did not defy society in any fundamental way. They were covert resisters and questioners of cultural values, while Kate Chopin openly attacked society. Her frankness doomed her, but it provided later generations of readers with exciting examples of overt resistance to the role of women in society.

The central theme in the fiction of Spofford, Freeman, and Chopin is how the cultural Mary could incorporate aspects of the Eve and the independent woman into her personality and actions without suffering social disapproval. Most of the fictional women were, on the surface, respectable wives and mothers, but all of them wished for something more. They wanted to break out of the dominant image and explore multiple avenues to selfhood, avenues that allowed expression of sexuality and independence. The excitement of their collective fiction was in their presentation of heroines who searched, however unsuccessfully, for ways to achieve that new, unusual synthesis.

The most hackneyed novels, like their counterparts in the movies and on television, saw women in only one, predictable image. But even the writers who created complex, interesting women ultimately had them return to the fold. The cultural rules might bend temporarily, but they also sprung back into their previous form. Rarely in popular cultural formula fiction or movies have we seen women abandon their families, like Edna Pontelier, or light out for the territory, like Huck Finn. After the restless and unhappy woman expressed her difference, she returned home.

Women writers often faced the challenge of creating distinct female personalities. Since the identity of a woman, until recently, was more closely attuned to cultural role definitions than that of a man, the challenge often went unmet. This fact also explained the conspicuous lack of great heroines in fiction, created by either men or women. Women in real life in most cultures and in most time periods lived predictable lives; they could not fulfill the writer's wish for adventurous types or unusual life experiences.

It is really only in the psychologically oriented twentieth century that heroines became fashionable and frequent. The interior novel, the introspective searchings within the mind, became landscapes congenial to female character development. Women knew about thinking and reflecting; they were used to assessing dialogues and examining interpersonal relationships. Their social roles demanded it. In a century that valued the inward look, women were suddenly acceptable as heroines. Women writers, sensitive to the changing tastes of their readers, responded with novels featuring the inner searchings of a desperate housewife or the internal monologue of a woman going mad.

The women's liberation movement in the 1970s required its fictional expression, and women writers seized the opportunity. While Spofford, Freeman, and Chopin wrote during a period when the women's suffrage movement struggled for success against obdurate resistance from both sexes, writers like Lois Gould and Sue Kaufman in the 1970s era found a large, sympathetic female audience. Suffrage for women was still not a respectable topic in the 1880s and 1890s when Chopin wrote her graphic descriptions of female sexuality. But women of all classes in the 1970s bought the paperback novels that described their emotional helplessness and their sexual longings. *Such Good Friends* (1970) catapulted Lois Gould into prominence as a writer, while *Fear of Flying* (1974) became a runaway bestseller, and author Erica Jong, who preferred to be known as a poet, became a nationally known figure.

The 1980s women's novels developed into a different genre than their 1970s predecessors. Many 1970s women writers were as much captives to popular convention as were earlier generations: the popular marketplace still determined the nature of much of their fiction. By definition, this is in the nature of popularity and of achieving popularity. While all generations of writers, if they wish to be popular, must forge connections with their audience, the 1970s writers created an unexpected popular formula: they invented overt resistance heroines (ostensibly a new type) who voluntarily accepted cultural formulas at the novel's end (an old form). Their Eves became Marys at the conclusion of the story. No longer were fictional women covertly resisting the bonds of society; they openly challenged them, but, and this a big but, they did not remain defiant at the end, as do some of the heroines of Freeman and Chopin. They meekly, willingly, and consciously accepted social definitions of their happiness. Isadora Wing in *Fear of Flying* returned to her psychiatrist-husband after her sexual misadventures; so do most of the women in most of the 1970s fiction.

The new formula appeared to be a reworking of a very old one: love and romance in the form of a good man still determined a woman's happiness, her reason for being, and her identity. In all of these "new" women's novels, the heroine had a moment of awakening when she realized, with horror, how her dreams, her habits, and her roles have been programmed for her and imposed upon her. She never had been the master of her own fate; she had been fated. The rest of the novel described her ramblings, her odyssey in search of truth, and her final reconciliation—which usually meant finding a new lover.

These novels still operated within the familiar woman's novel formula. Heroine met lover, rejected him for indeterminate reasons, sought experience, returned to lover. The primary difference with these so-called feminist novels was the frank discussions of woman's sexual longings and behavior. Further, the vocabulary of these novels contained words such as liberation, self-searching, and individual potential. The words gave it a false sense of newness. Actually, these novels do no more than Mary Wilkins Freeman or Kate Chopin did. While Freeman's women defied society in respectable ways and still remained, at least on the surface, social participators, Chopin's women broke social rules and boldly proclaimed their sexual happiness as the greatest good. An examination of current novels found no additional ground broken, no new barriers surmounted. Most of the contemporary women writers were closer to Chopin than Freeman, but they were not beyond either of them.

In the 1980s, there has been an amazing resurgence of gothic romance novels. Harlequin and multiple imitators produced literally hundreds of weekly fictions in which the virginal heroine waited for Mr. Right before experiencing the joys of sex. Occasionally, she was a career woman (an independent woman), but almost always she gladly abandoned her independence for the man of her dreams. The popular feminist novels of the 1970s have spawned the traditional, unfeminist romances of the 1980s.

The brilliant way that the popular nineteenth century women writers synthesized acceptable and subversive themes in their writing was absent in most current women's fiction. Mary Wilkins Freeman believed that society existed, its rules had to be obeyed to insure social stability, and that women's lives, though strained by those rules, had to live within them. The tension, strain, and struggle between individual will and social necessity were portrayed and respected, though ultimately society had to win the struggle. The Mary, Eve, and independent woman images appeared, but usually in socially acceptable ways.

The 1970s women writers rejected society as a viable entity, discarded rules altogether as binding human forces, and focused upon the smallest social unit, the family, as the source of all tension and frustration. This theme persisted in many 1980s novels as well. Today mothers are blamed for daughters' aggravations. Heroines face the difficult task of separating themselves from their loving mothers. Susan Fromberg Schaeffer, who has been a prolific writer during the past decade, introduced the puzzle of family relations in her early book, *Falling* (1973). Her heroine rebelled against her parents only to return home and marry a respectable man. "Parents and children," she concluded, "it was an impossible riddle."

To escape from the mother she loves-hates, the heroine in much of contemporary women's fiction sought a sympathetic lover, a man who could become parent and husband, protector and provider. But the same scenario inevitably ensued: he was then perceived as the parent she was rejecting, and the heroine moved on to different people, different adventures, always hoping against hope that the hate side of the dialectic would disappear. The heroine sought external sources of comfort, external explanations for her unhappiness. There was no stoicism, no inner questioning, no soul searching in these novels. There were no Mary Wilkins Freeman heroines who endured their lot and then carved out respectable human lives from adversity.

Sociofiction is an apt description of contemporary novels by women, a form of writing that delineated the author's personal experiences minutely, sharing with the reader 'what it was like' living in suburbia in the 1950s, 1960s, and 1970s, what the discussions were at a cocktail party in Cambridge or Long Island, and in graphic detail, the pleasures and horrors of sexual meetings. Marilyn French's popular *Women's Room* (1977), Silvia Tennenbaum's *Rachel, the Rabbi's Wife* (1978), and most recently Sue Miller's *The Good Mother* (1986) are all examples of personal chronicles. While the tone of French's book was bitter and antimale, both Tennenbaum and Miller were more sympathetic to both sexes. Miller's divorced mother was more stoical, but also a slave to her own failings. There was compassion in all three novels for the woman's struggle to become independent, but all three qualify as a sociological description of women's unhappy lives in the age of liberation, more than an imaginative, literary study of both a particular and universal·subject. They echo contemporary sociological discussions of how women can have it all (Mary/Eve/independent woman), but they do not create sympathetic fictional heroines, nor do they offer fictive solutions.

While Mary Wilkins Freeman disguised the discontent of her heroines and accentuated their strength and moral certitude, Erica Jong and her followers emphasized the weaknesses of heroines, proclaimed their complaints, and described their longings. Self-sacrificing heroines and stoical women who endured and prevailed have been replaced with loud sufferers. The greater the failings, the surer the success. Especially in the 1970s, women's fiction exposed vulnerability and no longer defined or defended strength. In 1980s popular romance, on the other hand, long-suffering heroines endured as they do on television melodramas. Indeed, there is no identifiable group of women novelists in the late 1980s that addresses any of these issues. Sociofiction has been replaced by individualistic expressions.

It is in other parts of popular culture that one can find resilient heroines and socially conscious ones as well. While popular fiction in recent years has created neither overt nor covert resisters, the movies, television, and popular music have been arenas in which women have experimented with, and experienced, new role possibilities.

NOTES

1. See James D. Hart, *The Popular Book: A History of America's Literary Taste* (Berkeley: University of California Press, 1963). A number of recent studies have explored women's novels of the nineteenth century from a feminist perspective; among them are Nina Baym, *Woman's Fiction: A Guide to Novels by and about Women in America, 1820–1870* (Ithaca, N.Y.: Cornell University Press, 1978) and Mary Kelley, *Private Woman, Public Stage: Literary Domesticity in Nineteenth Century America* (New York: Oxford University Press, 1984).

2. Quoted in Kathleen Conway McGrath, "Popular Literature as Social Reinforcement: The Case of *Charlotte Temple*," in *Images of Women in Fiction*, ed. Susan Koppelman Cornillon (Bowling Green: Bowling Green University Press, 1973, rev. ed.), p. 21.

3. A summary of her life and work can be found in Elizabeth K. Halbeisen, *Harriet Prescott Spofford: A Romantic Survival* (Philadelphia: University of Pennsylvania Press, 1935).

4. Ibid., p. 80.

5. Harriet Prescott, "Desert Sands," in *The Amber Gods and Other Stories* (Boston: Ticknor & Fields, 1863), pp. 182–83.

6. Ibid., p. 114.

7. Harriet Prescott Spofford, *An Inheritance* (New York: Charles Scribner and Son, 1897), p. 166.

8. Harriet Prescott, *Azarian: An Episode* (Boston: Ticknor and Fields, 1864).

9. Ibid., p. 232.

10. Ibid., pp. 237–38.

11. Ibid., pp. 246–47.

12. Ibid., p. 248.

13. Harriet Prescott Spofford, "Jo and I," *Harper's New Monthly Magazine*, March 1874, pp. 562–72.

14. Harriet Prescott Spofford, "Mrs. Hetty's Husband," *Cosmopolitan*, May 1886, pp. 135–42.

15. Mary Wilkins Freeman, "A New England Nun," *The Best Stories of Mary Wilkins Freeman*, comp. Henry W. Lanier (New York: Harper and Brothers, 1927), p. 71.

16. Ibid.

17. Mary Wilkins Freeman, "The Revolt of Mother," *A New England Nun and Other Stories* (Ridgewood, N.J.: Gregg Press, 1967).

18. Mary Wilkins Freeman, "A Humble Romance," in *Best Stories*, pp. 1–22.

19. Ibid., p. 168.

20. Ibid.

21. Mary Wilkins Freeman, "The Gospel According to Joan," in *Best Stories*, p. 465.

22. See the introduction by Per Seyersted in the two-volume collection, *The Complete Works of Kate Chopin* (Baton Rouge: Louisiana State University Press, 1969).

23. Kate Chopin, *The Awakening and Other Stories* (New York: Holt, Rinehart and Winston, 1970), p. 121.

24. Kate Chopin, *Complete Works*, vol. 1, p. 469.

25. Ibid., pp. 204–11.

26. Ibid., p. 206.

27. Ibid., vol. 2, pp. 592–96.

28. Ibid., pp. 594–95.

29. Ibid., p. 596.

30. Kate Chopin, *The Awakening*, p. 257.

31. Ibid., p. 297.

32. Ibid., p. xvii.

3

Filmic Images of Women

Until television overtook them, movies were the favorite visual entertainment in the United States. Fully half of the population, 60 million people, went to the movies each week during the 1930s. Because it was a period of economic depression, people needed the enjoyment, the escape, and the fantasy of films more than ever. The 1930s and 1940s became Hollywood's Golden Era. Among the hundreds of movies produced by the big studios each year, women were featured both in the very popular romance-melodramas and in the newer form, the independent woman films. Often, there were creative mergers: romance combined with independence and Eve types displayed strength and assertiveness. The newer type of film, however, had stronger women playing stronger parts in greater quantity than ever before, or possibly since.

The fantasy power of movies operated at full throttle. Precisely when the Depression created mass insecurity, vivacious women in film were surviving and taking control of difficult situations. As independent Eves, they used their physical attractiveness to carve out decent lives for themselves; as careerists, they became pilots, illustrators, reporters, doctors, lawyers, and businesswomen. And as aristocratic women whose family fortunes gave them unprecedented freedom, they often demonstrated, comically or melodramatically, some of the dilemmas of wealth; after all, women were not expected to function alone as adults. Hollywood also reveled in the opportunity to satirize the rich while clearly showing them in enviable positions. Aristocratic women paraded around in sumptuous surroundings while the masses were unemployed. In *My Man Godfrey* (1936), a classic screwball comedy, Carole Lombard and her socialite friends went to a charity treasure hunt. Lombard won the prize by bringing back a real life bum. In *The Women* (1939) rich New York City women were ridiculed for their useless lives, while a lengthy fashion show punctuated the middle section of the movie.

It is an interesting cultural statement that in the classless United States, during the bleak days of the Great Depression, moviegoers were treated to films about rich women. Many movies showed country homes, servants galore, and gorgeously dressed hostesses presiding over classy cocktail parties. The conspicuous signs of wealth in a country that preached egalitarianism appeared ironic indeed. Yet these films produced no revolutions; audiences enjoyed them and kept coming back for more. Their dreamlike qualities seemed to provide the needed escape. The U.S. public accepted the myth of everyone being equal while knowing full well that it was a myth. Blacks were not equal to whites, and rich people were different from everyone else. But Hollywood's movies about wealthy people in the United States were very popular in the 1930s.

The major studios of Hollywood each produced about 200 movies a year during that period. They satisfied an audience of all ages and races. There were family movies as well as special interest movies for every taste. Actresses found roles, as stars and in supporting roles, in most of Hollywood's offerings, though they were featured in romance-melodramas and independent women films. A generation of female movie stars arose to meet this seemingly insatiable appetite for movies. The list of women who became stars in the 1930s and 1940s cannot be rivalled by any subsequent generation of movie stars, primarily because there are no longer such large numbers of movies made each year. While Bette Davis, under long-term contract to Warner Brothers, often made three or four movies a year during the 1930s, a movie star in the post–1950 generation would be lucky to make one movie every two or three years. Joan Crawford, another star of the era, worked for MGM during the 1930s and made 29 movies during the decade.

While the 1930s generation of women actresses played in all of the standard fare—westerns, gangster movies, melodramas, and comedies—they also starred in the variations of independent women films. This role featured a heroine who was often restless and spent a lot of time discovering herself, though she usually ended up defining herself in terms of romance and marriage. The independent woman was also the working girl who found life bleak during the depression; her only path to future security and happiness was in the arms of a rich man. This film genre, in its variety, distinguished itself from the other types by featuring women, especially strong women, whose personal quest seemed to personify everyone's search for answers in very trying times. Indeed, this may have been part of its appeal; audiences were treated to unsettled times with a woman, usually the traditional anchor of the home, thrust into a new life situation. The resolution, with her returning to the home, offered assurances to both sexes that the difficult, and unusual, times would eventually be righted. The status quo ante depression would be restored.

Another characteristic of the independent woman film that marked it off from the other types was its singular focus upon the dilemma of a woman, not of a man or a family. In 1928, in the silent movie starring Joan Crawford as a yearning flapper, *Our Dancing Daughters*, the type was anticipated. Our heroine jumped upon a table during a party, raised her champagne glass, and toasted herself: "To myself, I have to live with myself until I die. So I hope I like myself."[1] Like her literary counterparts, the independent woman sought her own identity, sometimes accommodating herself to social pressures and sometimes not. In one of the most unusual endings of an independent woman film, Bette Davis's *Marked Woman* (1937), she refused the attention and protection of district attorney Humphrey Bogart and walked off, arms linked with her prostitute-colleagues. But even in the majority of movies with conventional endings, the important part was the middle with the expected ending being tacked on to soothe the hopes of society for an orderly and knowable world.

Though many movie actresses played in this genre, Katharine Hepburn and Rosalind Russell are probably the most clearly identified as exemplars of independent women. In the period under discussion, 1930–50, Hepburn played in five career woman films and four aristocratic women films, while Russell was a career woman seven times and an aristocratic lady three times (see table). Other popular stars of the period, Barbara Stanwyck, Bette Davis, and Joan Crawford, though often known for their work in romance and melodrama, also played many roles where their strength, independence, and grit were critical factors. They demonstrated some of the varieties of independent women. Careerists were portrayed along with aristocratic ladies and independent Eves. Hepburn was never an Eve. Her screen roles were the most consistent as she never entered into a long-term contract with any studio, in contrast to most other actresses. Bette Davis and Joan Crawford, as already suggested, did not have the luxury of choosing roles, but their personalities and talents lent themselves to roles about unusual women.

A selective description of independent woman roles played by Hepburn, Russell, Stanwyck, Davis, and Crawford illustrates the variety, as well as the consistency, of this image during the heyday of Hollywood. A group of other stars and their movies could easily be compiled, but these five stars constitute an impressive group who enjoyed long and successful careers and who made, amongst them, hundreds of movies. Of the three living members of the group (Hepburn, Davis, and Stanwyck), Hepburn is still featured occasionally in popular magazines, and Stanwyck had a second career on television, first in "The Big Valley" during the 1950s and more recently on "The Colbys." Together, these actresses played most of the variations of the independent woman image.

In *A Woman Rebels* (1936), Katharine Hepburn played the part of Pamela Thistlewaite, an upper-class Englishwoman who bridled against her teacher's statement that women were inferior. She refused to study "Mrs. Ellis' Guide to Ladyhood" because she considered its message rubbish. Despite her rebelliousness, Pamela succumbed to the charms of a caddish aristocrat, who failed to tell her that he was already married. Pregnant and unmarried, Pamela left England for a visit with her married sister in Italy. A series of events followed that could only occur in a movie: her sister Flora, also pregnant, lost her baby upon hearing the news that her husband was killed at sea; Pamela agreed to let Flora have her baby, but Flora died soon after, and Pamela returned to England with her child, pretending that it was her niece. She then became a fiery writer, editor, and lecturer on women's rights while raising her daughter. Portrayed as an effective but unloving woman, Pamela disguised her affection for Flora (she named her daughter after her dead sister). In the end, Flora learned the truth, and mother and daughter reconciled. Pamela was also united with her long-faithful love (whom she had met in Italy early in the film), Thomas Lane, played by Herbert Marshall. "These modern women are so weak," Lane concluded, and Pamela commented, as she embraced him, "Aren't they?" Once again, at least in the final reel, love leveled the able, independent womanly spirit, but until then, Pamela Thistlewaite exhibited the traits of an admirable reformer.

The film that most richly defined the perils of independence for women was *Woman of the Year*, a 1942 MGM offering that starred Hepburn and Spencer Tracy in their first team effort. Hepburn played Tess Harding, international journalist, speaker of many languages, party giver, and converser with the elite. Tracy was Sam Craig, the sportswriter on the same newspaper for which Tess Harding wrote her brilliant political commentary. Done as a comedy, role reversal became the comic tool. Harding as a careerist, an admittedly unusual role for a woman, was hardworking, driving, and serious. Craig's work meant baseball games and barrooms, seemingly frivolous and unimportant. While he was thoughtful, considerate, conventional, she initiated the romance, pursued it, and finally won him over. He insisted upon wearing formal garb at their wedding; he called his mother, got a recipe book from her, and assumed that their marriage would be traditional. Once married, Tess ignored him and went about her business of living an exciting professional life. They learned, at one point in the movie, that they both had been in Chicago at the same time, he for a

A Sample of Independent Woman Films, 1930–1950

Katharine Hepburn	as careerist	1933	A Bill of Divorcement
		1933	Christopher Strong
		1936	A Woman Rebels
		1941	Woman of the Year
		1949	Adam's Rib
	as aristocrat	1938	Holiday
		1938	Bringing Up Baby
		1940	The Philadelphia Story
		1943	Keeper of the Flame
Barbara Stanwyck	as careerist	1941	You Belong to Me
		1947	The Other Love
	as aristocrat	1937	Breakfast for Two
		1938	The Mad Miss Manton
		1946	My Reputation
		1946	The Strange Love of Martha Ivers
		1948	B.F.'s Daughter
		1949	East Side, West Side
	as Independent Eve	1939	Golden Boy
		1940	Remember the Night
		1941	The Lady Eve
		1946	California
		1950	No Man of Her Own
Joan Crawford	as careerist	1933	Dancing Lady
		1945	Mildred Pierce
		1947	Daisy Kenyon
	as aristocrat	1934	Forsaking All Others
		1935	I Live My Life
		1946	Humoresque
	as Independent Eve	1932	Rain
		1934	Sadie McKee
		1938	Mannequin
		1939	The Shining Hour
Rosalind Russell	as careerist	1938	The Citadel
		1940	His Girl Friday
		1940	Hired Wife
		1942	Take a Letter, Darling
		1943	Flight for Freedom
		1943	What a Woman
		1946	She Wouldn't Say Yes
	as aristocrat	1936	Craig's Wife
		1936	Trouble for Two
		1938	Man-Proof
Bette Davis	as careerist	1933	Ex-Lady
		1935	Front Page Woman
		1935	Dangerous
		1945	The Corn Is Green
		1950	All About Eve
	as aristocrat	1939	Dark Victory
		1942	Now, Voyager
	as Independent Eve	1933	20,000 Years in Sing-Sing
		1934	Of Human Bondage
		1935	Bordertown
		1937	Marked Woman
		1938	Jezebel

football game and she for a political meeting, but neither discovered this fact until both had returned to New York. He was upset that she did not call him at the press room to arrange a meeting, while she could not understand why he was so perturbed. The critical moment and turning point of the film came when Tess surprised her husband with a Greek refugee boy whom she had agreed to raise. Her motives, however, were not maternal; she had been co-chairman of the Greek Refugee Committee and felt obligated to be the first to volunteer her home for a needy child. Her husband objected because of her motives and because he wanted a child of their own. But he relented and the child was taken into their home.

Tess continued to pursue her career avidly. Sam left her and, in the final scene where she sought a reconciliation, she entered his kitchen, a room with which she was unfamiliar, and prepared breakfast for him. Tess Harding, the able political columnist, burnt the toast, watched the water boil out, and saw the cereal sputter all over the stove. Her noisy activity brought her husband to the kitchen. Tess, reduced to tears of frustration, agreed with him that she did not have to be all things to all people—neither Mrs. Craig nor Tess Harding—but rather Tess Harding Craig. Ostensibly, the case for a woman's career was vindicated in *Woman of the Year*. However, how she was going to reconcile both roles remained unexplained and unexplored. How, indeed, was she to pursue a time-consuming career while keeping house and raising children? Yet the very fact that a 1942 movie featured a successful, married career woman made it very special.

The fantasy and conventional needs of U.S. women and men must surely have been satisfied in *Woman of the Year*. Women were pleased to see a sophisticated woman stand up to a man, while men were happy to note her conformity at the end. This movie was a very good example of how the independent woman film offered comfort to both sexes during the depression. Women enjoyed watching Katharine Hepburn meet people from all over the world; they might fantasize about the possibilities of that kind of life while seeing her finally subdued and returned to the classic mold of wife. Even the exceptional woman accepted marriage as her supreme purpose. Men, similarly, could enjoy being in the presence of an "interesting" woman at the same time that they saw her husband dominate her at the end. The status quo was not endangered. Yet for most of the movie Tess Harding lived a materially different life from the audience, thus providing them with rich fantasy experiences. The genius of *Woman of the Year* was its way of synthesizing the exciting life possibilities for women with the expected; everyone left the theater pleased, with the possible exception of Tess Harding.

Rosalind Russell epitomized the career woman in film. Indeed, she became so tired of the image that she left Hollywood for the stage. She later recalled:

In 19 pictures I played 19 different career women: a woman judge, a woman psychiatrist, a woman lawyer, a woman dean, a woman advertising executive. The rest are a blur.

In every picture I was supposed to be very crisp, intelligent, and sure of myself, the kind of woman that men universally abhor. In one picture, where I had supervisory charge of Fred MacMurray and 114 other men, reports came back that males across the land were angrily storming out of theaters in mid-picture. They should have waited until the happy ending. It was always the same. I got my comeuppance. . . . [2]

In one of her most popular examples of the type, *His Girl Friday* (1940), Russell played a reporter, divorced from editor Cary Grant and preparing to marry staid insurance salesman Ralph Bellamy. But the desire to get a major story before chucking the exciting life of reporting for marriage and a home in the suburbs kept her at the newspaper. Eventually, of course, she returned to the arms of her first love. Russell displayed the admirable traits of a self-assured woman: she was hard working, ambitious, and anxious to succeed. Though she kept talking about giving up the dog–eat–dog world of journalism for domesticity, in the end she did not. As did Hepburn in *Woman of the Year*, Russell in *His Girl Friday* embraced her lover at the end, and the viewer was given the impression that career and marriage could be reconciled somehow.

Reporters were favorite professions for women in the films of the 1930s. There were only about 15,000 real-life women journalists, but the famous ones such as Dorothy Thompson, Martha Gellhorn, and Anne O'Hare McCormick were well known to women in the United States. On the screen, women viewers enjoyed seeing their favorite stars play the part of reporter. Though romance and marriage occupied their minds, they showed themselves to be fearless, exciting, and able to compete effectively in a man's world. The intriguing quality of the career woman movies was that they raised the very modern theme of career and marriage for women; in the preliberation era of the 1930s and 1940s, the theme had to be treated comically because its serious implications were beyond the culture's imagination at that point.

Take a Letter, Darling (1942) offered movie viewers an excellent chance to laugh at the U.S. businesswoman. In a classic role reversal situation, Rosalind Russell as A. M. MacGregor, dynamic advertising executive, hired Tom Verney played by Fred MacMurray as her social secretary. MacGregor had started eight years before as a secretary to Mr. Atwater and within a few years became a partner. Her drive, ability, and enthusiasm for her work made her inimitable. In dealing with her male clients, though, dinner parties were often necessary, and jealous wives were ever present. Thus, MacGregor found that a male social secretary posing as her fiancé, was essential to assuage the anxiety of her clients' wives. Most men, however, did not last long in the position as they became romantically interested in their boss. "A woman in business faces many problems that men don't face," MacGregor reminded her new employee, "in fact one of them is men."

Artist Tom Verney, in need of money so that he can go off to Mexico and paint, took the job reluctantly. After a series of improbable turns, the plot finally reached its happy conclusion: MacGregor gave up her career and went to Mexico with her struggling hero. True love surmounted the allure of New York City, other romantic interests, and exciting work. Again, the dichotomy, marriage or a career, was demanded of the heroine. Predictably and dutifully, she chose marriage as all red-blooded U.S. women did. The businesswoman was characterized as "beautiful brain, beautiful clothes, no temperature, no pulse." Although MacGregor appeared warm and charming throughout, the majority of males felt that, because she was a successful businesswoman, she was cold, hard, and aggressive, traits positively assigned to successful men. To movie producers and their audiences of the 1940s, women gladly sacrificed their personal ambitions for the love of a good man. But again, except for the ending, A. M. MacGregor was in charge. The old roles for women, side by side with glimpses of new possibilities, entertained the audiences in such films.

The independent Eve projected a very different kind of independent woman. She was often a marginal woman who survived through guile as well as natural beauty. Barbara Stanwyck in *Golden Boy* (1939), for example, projected a grim but determined portrait of a woman who had learned how to survive in an unfriendly world. The movie, a boxing story, starred Stanwyck (Lorna Moore) with Adolphe Menjou (Tom Moody) as her promoter-boy friend and William Holden (Joe Bonaparte) in his first starring role as a violinist and boxer. When one of the toughs called Stanwyck "my girl," she retorted, "I'm not anyone's girl, I'm my mother's girl." Despite her display of independence, however, she depended upon Menjou whom she hoped to marry once his divorce became final. Because of her loyalty to Menjou, she used her feminine wiles to convince violinist Holden to box; "don't worry," she assured Menjou, "I'm a dame from Newark and I know a dozen ways." Predictably, Stanwyck fell in love with Holden, and so ended her cynicism.

As in most of the independent Eve films, Stanwyck was portrayed as a victim of circumstance, a working-class woman whose natural good looks saved her from the factory assembly line or clerking in a department store. Her life options were limited because of her class; she was not lucky enough to meet and marry a rich man, so she must make do. Her sex appeal became her major weapon in the game of life, and she used it realistically and knowingly. But true love surmounted self-interest. Stanwyck was willing to sacrifice her happiness and security for the man she loved, but she was repaid for her selflessness by winning both at the film's conclusion. Stanwyck's inner strength shone throughout *Golden Boy*, as it did in most of her films. Independent Eves may appear as disreputable to staid society, but they are also survivors in a hostile environment; they are independent by necessity and must learn how to cope. Though usually linked with a gangster, and viewed as his convenient sex object, when Stanwyck or Bette Davis took such a role, they created great sympathy for the Eve and admiration for her independence.

The Lady Eve (1941), a superb comedy that starred Stanwyck as a card shark, offered audiences a humorous depiction of the Adam and Eve struggle. Stanwyck, in a part that won her an Academy Award nomination, played Jean Harrington, who, with her father, played by Charles Coburn, rode the luxury ocean liners looking for innocent prey. On the initial voyage of the movie, their prospective conquest, played by Henry Fonda, was Charlie Pike, heir to a beer fortune. Pike was the perfect victim, an ornithologist more knowledgeable in the ways of birds than of people. During the course of the film, the Harringtons deceived him in a variety of ways; Jean passed herself off as two different women, marrying him under the guise of the second one only to reintroduce her original self at the end of the movie.

Jean Harrington was a woman who learned from her father how to live by her wits. However, pangs of love and conscience softened her will to deceive. In fact, throughout the film, her behavior revolved around her love/hate attitudes to Pike. When she loved him, she protected him against her father's card tricks; when she was angry with him, she participated in the trickery. A woman card shark, as seen in The Lady Eve (where the temptress theme from the Garden of Eden was graphically drawn at the beginning of the movie), was not consistently cold and professional at her work. True to Hollywood convention, love unnerved her; only when she was emotionally uninvolved coud she compete with the best of them.

Stanwyck as Jean Harrington fits the Eve image perfectly. She was sophisticated and all-knowing, while the man in her life was inexperienced, a male fantasy that has had a lot of mileage in Western culture. Women lured innocent men into evil doings; they were the sinners while Adams were the victims. At the same time that western mythology proclaimed male dominance, it subscribed to the theory of female sexual aggressiveness. A woman seduced a man; he would never have thought or acted out those feelings without her alluring actions. He is Adam and she is Eve. Innumerable variations on this theme were played out in the movies of the 1930s and 1940s, and indeed since then as well.

While Hepburn and Russell were the careerists and the aristocrats, and Stanwyck was the independent Eve par excellence, Bette Davis played all of these roles on screen. Her range was great, contrary to the impersonators' treatment of her in recent years. In Ex-Lady (1933), for example, her first starring role, she played Helen, a successful, independent commercial artist who was having a love affair with Don (Gene Raymond), an advertising agency owner. Helen sets the tone of the film early on: she loved her work and, despite Don's constant pleading, refused to marry him. She declared:

"No one has any rights about me except me."
"I don't want to get married."
"I don't want to be like my mother."
"Being married means doing what the other person wants. I don't want babies. I want to stay young. . . . Let's be lovers again and be separate persons."

Because Don persisted, and she did love him, they eventually married, and Helen went to work in his agency. Business pressures mounted and the marriage floundered. Helen proposed that they separate, maintain their own apartments once again, and meet when the spirit moved them. He agreed but this arrangement also had its problems, and at the end they decided that marriage, in one domicile, though difficult, is better than all other possible arrangements. Neither Helen nor Don gave up their careers; neither blamed the other for their past problems. They simply declared their love for each other and agreed to work at making their marriage effective.

The honesty of this film and its depiction of a strong, alluring woman who gave up none of her integrity in order to gain both the man she loved and her career were truly astounding. The exceptionality of *Ex-Lady*, of course, confirmed the dominant message of the movies and U.S. culture. It was especially rare for Hollywood in the 1930s to portray an autonomous, married woman. Bette Davis played Helen with great attractiveness, but *Ex-Lady* was not followed by any imitators of its unusual theme. Her subsequent movies sometimes allowed her to play independent women but not iconoclastic types like Helen.

Two years later, in *Front Page Woman*, Davis was a newspaper reporter. The film raised the question: Can a woman be a good newspaper reporter, or is she destined for homemaking? Star reporter Curt Devlin, played by George Brent, answered the question unequivocally early in the film; he told Ellen Garfield (Bette Davis), reporter for a rival newspaper, that she should give up reporting, marry him, and become a domestic. The whole film revolved around Ellen's efforts to prove to Curt that she was a good reporter. He bargained with her, however, and got her to agree that if she did not scoop him in a story she would give up the business and marry him. A juicy unsolved murder provided them with the material for action. Each tried to solve the murder, to discover the mystery weapon, get exclusive stories, and find out the decision of the jury before the other. The score was tied until the last round, when Curt spied on the jury, scooped the story, and then forged new jury ballots to deceive his lady love. Rather than express outrage at his shocking behavior, Ellen accepted her fate.

In the end, Curt admitted to Ellen that she was a damn good reporter, to which she replied: "Really, do you really mean that?" He assured her that he did and they embraced, sure to live happily ever after. His snide remarks to her throughout the movie were quickly forgotten: "I thought you would be out of the business and taking a course in domestic science by now" and "a woman's place is in the home." Only once did she respond spunkily: "When I do it, its luck, but when you do it, its being a good reporter." But her heart evidently was not in her remark. She conceded, won a pyrrhic victory, and retreated to the home—no more scoops, no more reporting of exciting events, no more meeting of interesting people. That's a man's business. Demure Ellen proved her point, *Front Page Woman* seemed to say, and that is all that was necessary. She could be a reporter, but that was not the truly significant purpose in her life; nor was it a full-time interest. Her love of her work took a back seat to domesticity.

Another star of U.S. movies, Joan Crawford, often played poor-but-honest women whose beauty won them a rich husband. Occasionally, she portrayed a career woman. In *Dancing Lady* (1933) she was a dancer whose love for dancing and whose ambition to succeed at it surpassed all else. As Jamie Barlow, Crawford exhibited all of the classic traits necessary for success in the opportunity-filled United States: she was hard working, perseverant, and self-confident. In the opening scene of the movie, she was a chorus girl in a low-class burlesque house; the place was raided and she was out of work. She met Todd Newton (Franchot Tone), a rich, spoiled playboy who took an interest in her. He wanted her to give up dancing and go away with him, but she asserted, quite emphatically, that dancing was the only life pursuit she wanted. Unbeknownest to Jamie, Newton bought into a major show, directed by Patch Gallagher (Clark Gable) and used his influence to secure her a job in it. Her willingness to work hard and her obvious talent convinced Patch that she was star material. Todd Newton, meanwhile, got Jamie to promise him that, if the show were not a success, she would leave show business and marry him. He then proceeded to subvert the show by taking his money out of the production. Eventually, the show was produced without Newton's money, Jamie starred, and the show became a success. She and Patch declared their mutual love, and Jamie ended up with her career and her lover, another rare example in movie history.

Crawford's strongest role, as a businesswoman in *Mildred Pierce* (1945), won her the only Academy Award of her career. Though it was a complex film with many different themes, a crucial one was that of a woman getting ahead on her own. Mildred Pierce started with nothing, and through hard work, guts, determination, and singlemindedness made a success of herself. The film explored the immense difficulties women have in our culture to be effective mothers while pursuing a career. It also showed the incredible poverty of goals that mothers had for their daughters in a materialistic society. Mildred Pierce wanted her two daughters to escape the humdrum of her life by taking dancing and piano lessons so that they could marry well and live a life of financial comfort.

Recently divorced Mildred Pierce assessed her strengths, decided that her cooking and baking talents could be translated into a business venture, and after working as a waitress, went into the restaurant business. She purchased an old home, turned it into a lovely, friendly, and personal restaurant and gave it the "feminine touch," even remembering customers' names after one or two meetings. After her first restaurant became successful, Mildred Pierce expanded into a chain of similar operations. After all, in the United States, a successful item was mass produced; she conformed to this well-established model, but her undoing was her romantic involvement with a weak playboy named Monte Beragon III (Zachary Scott). Monte supplied Mildred with an image of herself as a soft, appealing woman, to which she responded since her life had always been one of deprivation and unrest. He encouraged her when she spoiled her older daughter, Veda, played by Ann Blyth. Ultimately, Veda fell in love with Monte and killed him when he rejected her. Mildred Pierce's businesses failed, and she faced personal and financial ruin at film's end. The bleak climax was moderated by the appearance of Mildred's former husband at the police station. She, then, would not be alone; a man walked at her side, and she could face the future with some hope.

The message of *Mildred Pierce*, however, was clear: ambitious women beware. Neglecting a family will have catastrophic consequences. The presence of children, in a film about a successful businesswoman, changes the possibilities. While a dancer, or an artist, might conceivably be able to achieve both love and career, a mother's primary focus had to be on her children. *Mildred Pierce* also warned against spoiling children. Even when Mildred was a poor, struggling housewife, she indulged Veda. Indeed, this was one of the causes for the first marital rift. The financial success of Mildred Pierce only dramatized and exaggerated the self-indulgent traits of Veda; new cars, showy clothes, and snobbish behavior were now possible. If Mildred had remained poor, her daughter would have become a small, petty woman living on false delusions rather than a rich, spoiled one.

The ten films just described effectively demonstrate the dual power of the independent woman genre: the ability to raise new, unconventional questions about women's lives while assuring both sexes that traditional sex roles will be preserved. Audiences had it both ways during the period of Hollywood's greatest successes; they witnessed women living public lives while seeing them fall into the hero's arms at film's end. The multiple needs satisfied by the independent women films produced during the depression made them very popular. Audiences were introduced to new possibilities while being assured of the verities of the old patterns. What better way was there to illustrate the human wish for both the preservation of the old and experimentation with the new than to depict women as independent, though determined by love?

The power of these films also lies in their unspoken respect for the woman's search for self, a decidedly modern theme. Vital women sought their own lives, defined themselves in ways that satisfied them personally. This feature distinguished the genre from all others. Standard melodrama lacked this quality. Further, the independent woman films anticipated by many years themes that occupy contemporary woman: How can personal and professional happiness be achieved? Can career and marriage successfully be combined?

While Hollywood portrayed white women within the three dominant images already described, black actresses were assigned entirely different images: they were tragic mulattoes, mammys, or scatterbrains. A racially segregated nation did not allow beautiful black women to be featured in any movie, let alone be cast as Eves; they became tragic mulattoes, light-skinned women who were doomed because of their mixed blood. Nina Mae McKinney, for example, was an attractive black actress who aspired to a movie career. She was featured as the temptress in the all-black musical *Hallelujah* (1929). One reviewer described her as "the dynamic, vivacious girl of the colored underworld, who lives by her wits and enmeshes the males by her personality, sex appeal and dancing feet." He went on to call her the "Clara Bow of her race."[3] MGM's King Vidor production, an unusual venture for conservative Hollywood, was considered risky but possible since the movie had an all-black cast and was distributed simultaneously to black and white theaters around the country. After all, the sexy McKinney was not luring white men into sinful activity. White audiences, however, were not ready to see any beautiful black women in suggestive roles. The movie did not succeed at the box office, and the seemingly promising movie career of Nina Mae McKinney went nowhere.

The woman who personified the mammy, the most reassuring image for white audiences, was Hattie McDaniel. She played in scores of movies during the Golden Era and was loved by audiences for her humane portrayals. As one critic said, her servant role "became the literal mother figure."[4] McDaniel was Jean Harlow's sympathetic maid in *Saratoga* (1937), Barbara Stanwyck's surrogate mother in *The Mad Miss Manton* (1938), and the brave and self-sacrificing mammy in *Gone with the Wind* (1939), the movie that won her the Academy Award in 1940 for best supporting actress.[5] Rather than the award becoming the opportunity for new and better roles, McDaniel found it impossible to obtain any roles after 1940. She often had to defend her mammy portrayal to black critics. "Why should I complain about making seven thousand dollars a week playing a maid? If I didn't, I'd be making seven dollars a week actually being one!"[6] Yet she wished for variety and depth of screen roles, but none came her way.

While Hattie McDaniel's ample figure fit the image of the motherly and reassuring black servant, Lena Horne appeared in Hollywood as a latter-day Nina Mae McKinney, another beautiful, light-skinned black woman yearning for a movie career. MGM signed her to a long-term contract, the first such arrangement for a black actress, but the studio found it beyond its imagination to use her effectively without offending white (particularly southern) audiences. Because she was a singer, she played a singer in many movies and often had her part cut out of the film when it was shown in the South. "They didn't make me into a maid," she has said, "but they didn't make me anything else either. I became a butterfly pinned to a column singing away in Movieland."[7]

Butterfly McQueen best exemplified the scatterbrained maid image. With her high-pitched voice and seemingly hysterical manner, she was the distracted young servant in *Gone With the Wind* as well as the faithful servant in *Mildred Pierce*. She was tied to this image as completely as McDaniel was to the mammy and McKinney to the tragic mulatto. White audiences were comforted and assured by the predictability of the roles of black women. The only alternative in Hollywood was to ignore black women completely.

A comparison of women's filmic images of the Golden Era to the 1970s and 1980s reveals the truth of the French adage, "the more things change, the more they remain the same." The power of old images, the utter endurance of the old formulas, makes it extremely difficult to break out and transform the conventions. Barbra Streisand, a superstar of the 1960s, 1970s, and 1980s, would seem to be able to transcend the dominant images, if anyone could. But in only two of her recent films was she able to do so. Streisand won the 1968 Academy Award for her portrayal of Fanny Brice in *Funny Girl*. In 1972, in response to her own feelings and the women's liberation movement, she made *Up the Sandbox*, a movie based upon the feminist novel by Anne Roiphe. The movie was a box office failure. The daydreaming sequences of a frustrated homemaker did not appeal to audiences. She said of this role that she identified with her character Margaret: "There is a part of me that longs to stay home and be with my child.... but there is another part of me that needs a form of expression other than bearing children, just as there is another part of Margaret that feels love is not enough."[8] In the following year, however, Streisand starred in a rare example of a romance/independent woman film that preserved its integrity and transcended the traditional borders.

In *The Way We Were* (1973), student radical Katie Morosky (played by Barbra Streisand), begins the film as an independent, spunky young woman who is deeply committed to peace during the turbulent 1930s. She is an activist who demonstrates for her beliefs, writes articles, and makes unpopular speeches to the accompaniment of student derision. The romantic hero, Hubbell Gardiner, played by Robert Redford, is a popular, athletic, seemingly empty-headed counterpart to Streisand's seriousness. She calls him "America the beautiful." They do strike up a friendship, however, and it is discovered that he has literary ambitions. They part after college and do not see each other until a chance meeting during the war when he is on furlough. Katie is already deeply in love with him, but he is much slower to reciprocate. Eventually they marry, move to California where he becomes a successful film writer, and divorce when he is willing to buckle under to the anti-Communist harangues and investigations that plagued Hollywood after the war. Katie's leftist politics have remained a vitalizing principle in her life, and she cannot abide by his easy abandon of principle for self-interest. At the end of the film they meet on a street in New York in the 1960s where she is distributing pamphlets for an antiwar rally while he, and his second wife, enter a posh hotel.

The film is a true departure from the romantic tradition. It has the courage to separate the lovers and have them establish other lives with other people. It allows Katie to continue her principled commitment to radical social causes and to raise her children with a new husband sympathetic to her interests. In this movie, like only a few other in any decade, the end of the romance does not destroy either partner's life and does not end up with the woman either crying or dying. This movie stands alone in its separation from the long tradition of women's films. Indeed, the rich interaction, throughout the movie, of the romantic formula and the independent social activist type is unique. Neither theme loses out to the other; both retain their integrity. The presence of superstars Streisand and Redford assured the success of the film and was responsible for an atypical, transforming treatment of an old formula.

Alice Doesn't Live Here Anymore (1975) described the life of a recently widowed mother, played by Ellen Burstyn, who tried to make a new life for herself and her son. She discovered that her singing ambitions were unrealizable because of her limited talent. Thus, she turned to the attractive romantic lead, played by Kris Kristofferson, for comfort, security, and her future. If the movie honestly faced Alice's limited talent as the reason for her failure as a singer, Alice might have qualified as an advanced and serious treatment of an important subject; what, indeed, do ambitious women do who want to shape their own lives? If, like most women and men, the striver for independence discovered that she had limited marketable skills, how would she reconcile her dreams with realities?

However, the movie did not face this question. Rather, external reasons were offered for Alice's failure: the few opportunities for a cafe singer in the small Arizona town in which she lived and the perverse men she met when she did sing at a bar. Alice, if she had been self-confident, would have gotten into her broken-down station wagon and kept driving east until she found a more congenial environment. While the movie sounded like a relevant 1970s film with its theme of women's liberation, raising a child alone, and the alienation of city life, it ultimately failed as a serious exploration of that subject. Romance occupied the most time, and romantic tensions overtook all other considerations.

Other 1970s contributions to the romantic genre did not depart from the 1930s tradition. *An Unmarried Woman* (1978), *Turning Point* (1977), and *The Goodbye Girl* (1977) all fit neatly into the older category of romance: true romance fulfilled a woman's life, while failed romance or no romance made a woman miserable. In *An Unmarried Woman*, for example, the heroine, played by Jill Clayburgh, was rudely informed by her husband one day that he wanted a divorce and already had his second wife picked out. Some of the strongest scenes in the movie showed Clayburgh adjusting to her new life with the aid of her female friends, a new feature of women's films of the 1970s. The movie became conventional, however, when it resolved her identity crisis by introducing her to a handsome artist, played by Alan Bates. He restored her self-confidence and became her source for future happiness.

In *Goodbye Girl*, the heroine, played by Marsha Mason, was an unmarried woman raising a child alone after her latest lover abandoned her. She tried to resume her dancing career but finds she is too out of shape. She is forlorn and saved by an actor who comes to claim the apartment in which she lives. They live together, fall in love, and she is transformed from a crying incompetent to a possessive, sometimes hysterical romantic. *Goodbye Girl* is a complete regression to the worst of the 1930s domestic comedies. The Mason character is unsympathetic and unattractive, and the viewer wonders why the actor, played brilliantly by Richard Dreyfuss, would spend two minutes with this unpleasant woman. Once again, the only claim to relevance or contemporariness is the frank discussion of an unmarried woman, in this case, one with a precocious, streetwise, and sassy daughter.

In the 1980s there have been few women's movies and few women movie stars of note. While the 1970s was not too sure how to deal with the new social reality called the women's movement, the 1980s seems determined to ignore the subject entirely. Indeed, as a commentator on the treatment of blacks in film has noted, when black leaders objected to the image portrayed on the screen, Hollywood filmmakers responded by eliminating the stereotypes—and erasing them from film altogether.[9] A similar phenomenon seems to operate regarding women's films during an era that criticized the traditional images. There is no generation of movie stars, quantitatively or qualitatively, to replace the Golden Age generation; inextricably tied to this fact is the absence of large numbers of movies featuring women. The old images no longer seem appropriate, but no new syntheses have been successful in replacing them.

Except for Meryl Streep, there is no great new movie star to rival Bette Davis, Katharine Hepburn, Joan Crawford, and Greta Garbo. There are few, if any, romances. To examine this phenomenon, and test this thesis, let us look at the film careers of two superstars of the contemporary generation who began their careers in the 1960s: Jane Fonda and Barbra Streisand. How have the recent years treated them?

A brief survey of both of their earlier careers is appropriate. Fonda has made over 30 movies; she has gone from playing the sweet Mary in *Tall Story* (1960) to many examples of the Eve image, such as the early *Walk on the Wild Side* (1962) to *Any Wednesday* (1966), culminating in *Klute* (1971). During the first part of the 1970s, Jane Fonda was considered box office poison because of her real life social activism. Critic Pauline Kael had assumed, in the early 1970s, that "Jane Fonda stands a good chance of personifying American tensions and dominating our movies in the 70s as Bette Davis did in the thirties."[10] But Fonda's work in the anti-Vietnam movement had turned the Hollywood establishment against her.

It was not until the comedy *Fun with Dick and Jane* in 1977 that she regained her popularity. The cinematic image of a relaxed, easygoing woman, willing to play for laughs, erased the real life image of the sober revolutionary. Fonda's subsequent movies in the late 1970s possessed a more consistent independent woman image. In *Julia* (1977) and *Comes a Horseman* (1978), she was cast as a writer and a brave frontierswoman respectively, while in *China Syndrome* (1979) and *Electric Horseman* (1979), she played reporters. But 1980 brought *Nine to Five*, a comedy in which she was overshadowed by her costars, Lily Tomlin and Dolly Parton. The following year saw her in *On Golden Pond*, a sentimental film about aging that featured her father, Henry Fonda, and Katharine Hepburn. She made no movies for the next five years but rather seemed to concentrate on her very successful exercise books and videotapes. Indeed, she entered, and captured, another popular arena: the public's love for how-to books and videos, in this case, exercise and physical fitness.

As already suggested, Streisand's star quality has shown in multimedia. Her great talent as a singer, a comedian, and an actress has earned her awards on Broadway, television, the movies, and in the record industry. She has made many musicals including *Hello Dolly* (1970) and *On a Clear Day* (1970), two successful comedies, *The Owl and the Pussycat* (1970) and *What's Up Doc?* (1972), the failed feminist film already mentioned, *Up the Sandbox* (1972), and the inimitable *The Way We Were* (1973). Though she has made six movies since, none tested her great ability or promised greater things than *Yentl* (1983).

Yentl was an audacious combination of the musical and the independent woman genre. Set in Eastern Europe at the turn of the century, *Yentl* tells the story of an intellectually curious young Jewish woman who yearns to study religious texts; unfortunately, the orthodox Jewish tradition did not allow women to do so. In order to overcome this inhibition, Yentl disguises herself as a young man. She subsequently falls in love with a fellow student while his betrothed falls in love with her. The movie explores the feminist question: how does society decide its division of rights and roles? It demonstrates the accepted prejudices against women in its treatment of Yentl disguised as a male versus Yentl as a female. Interspersed with the serious probing of these issues are Yentl's musical musings. The unusual format of *Yentl* and the difficulty some critics had with considering Streisand as a young man affected its reception. While audiences liked it, and the movie did especially well abroad and on videotape, the critics did not and the Motion Picture Academy ignored it.

The uniqueness of *Yentl*, which amply displayed Streisand's abundant talents, was difficult to categorize; subsequently, it puzzled many viewers. Streisand's innovative interest in borrowing from the musical, the romance, and the independent woman film formulas, plus the fact that she wrote, directed, produced, and starred in the film, made it an audacious and exciting movie, but one that was not fully appreciated. Surely, the setting in an Eastern European community did not increase interest. Further, musicals made for a mature, adult audience, as opposed to rock musical movies for teenagers, seem to have lost their market. The movie audiences in the 1980s is young, and the sentimental ballads of *Yentl*, as well as her intellectual yearnings, did not appeal to the youth of this country. Another cultural statement.

Streisand recognized that the success or failure of *Yentl* had far-reaching implications. She told one interviewer: "If I failed, not only would the film fail, I would set back the cause of women. A man can fail, and nobody says, 'We won't hire any more men.' But let a woman fail, and it hurts all women."[11] Streisand recognized the interaction between her screen roles and her persona; she knew that she was a celebrity whose personal and public lives were closely watched and commented upon. When trying to break out of the old stereotypes, she was criticized and feared the repercussions for other women in the movie business.

New syntheses are clearly called for, but the times make it difficult. Marys are no longer viable unless they combine with independent women qualities or express their latent Eve traits. Independent women are dangerous if they resemble real life feminists. And Eves appear irrelevant in the sexually liberated 1980s. Surely, creative thinkers can imagine clever variations and mixtures of these images. But their efforts have been noticeably absent of late.

NOTES

1. All of the films discussed in this chapter are representative of the corpus of films called "independent women" films. I have viewed virtually all the films of Hepburn, Crawford, Davis, Russell, and Stanwyck.

2. Rosalind Russell, "What I've learned about men," *American Magazine*, August 1953, p. 101.

3. Mark, "Hallelujah," *Variety*, August 28, 1929, reprinted in *Variety Film Reviews 1926–1929*, vol. 3 (New York: Garland, 1983), unpaged.

4. Donald Bogle, *Toms, Coons, Mulattoes, Mammies and Bucks: An Interpretive History of Blacks in American Films* (New York: Viking Press, 1973), p. 82.

5. Leonard J. Leff, "The Search for Hattie McDaniel," *New Orleans Review*, vol. 10, nos. 2/3, 1983, p. 92.

6. Bogle, *Toms, Coons, Mulattoes*, p. 82.

7. Lena Horne and Richard Schickel, *Lena* (New York: Doubleday, 1965), p. 135.

8. James Spada, ed., *Barbra, The First Decade: The Films and Career of Barbra Streisand* (Secaucus, N.J.: Citadel Press, 1974), pp. 153–54.

9. Leff, "Hattie McDaniel," p. 92.

10. Quoted in Martin Kasindorf, "Fonda, A Person of Many Parts," *New York Times Magazine*, February 3, 1974, p. 20.

11. Bob Thomas's interview with Barbra Streisand, *San Diego Union*, January 6, 1984.

4

Women Movie Stars as Role Models

As already suggested in the Introduction, fans of the women entertainers read all about them. During the 1930s, *Modern Screen*, *Photoplay*, and *Motion Picture* were among the fan magazines that enjoyed wide circulation. The personal as well as professional lives of the stars received attention. Their childhood histories and their marital histories were described in detail. In this way, the followers gained a sense of knowledge and familiarity that enabled them to incorporate their favorite actresses into their circle of acquaintances. In recent years, researchers of the fans of soap opera stars have noted the same phenomenon.[1]

The movie stars became role models to their female fans in many senses: the fans demonstrated their admiration and loyalty by attending all of their favorite stars' movies and buying whatever product they endorsed. Peroxide sales went up when Jean Harlow became a blonde; fashions, especially by designer Adrian who dressed Joan Crawford in all of her films, were copied for the masses. Further, though impossible to document fully, it is also conceivable to imagine that people identified with the suffering of their favorite star and connected it to their own travails. The actresses, in this sense, provided a constructive model of how to survive adversity, how to develop self-confidence, and how to take control of one's life.

We know about the lives of the female actresses by reading the same magazines read by the fans. The juicy stories usually appeared in each and every feature about the person. Every time a new film appeared, the press office of the studio flooded the magazines and newspapers with stories on the movie and the players, a practice still in effect today. While studios served as a major supplier of information about their "properties," magazine reporters also sought out the most popular stars for interviews. Gossip columnists like Hedda Hopper and Louella Parsons supplied readers with inside scoops as well. Collectively, these sources created a rich variety of gossip, rumor, and partial truth, material that was avidly consumed by the magazine buyers. The validity of the stories mattered less than the vitality of the news.

Often, the actresses contributed to the excitement by doing unusual or outrageous things. Magazine readers delighted in learning that Rosalind Russell greased her hair with vaseline in preparation for her meeting with studio chief Carl Laemmele in the early 1930s. Russell had wanted to end her contract with Universal Studios and decided to appear as unglamorous as possible at the renewal meeting. She succeeded. Russell's reputation as a shrewd businesswoman, on and off the screen, became well known and prompted one Hollywood reporter to write, "In Hollywood, Rosalind Russell is regarded as the one star who has done more to make women with brains popular." Carole Lombard staged innumerable comic antics, swore like a sailor, which even surprised some veteran Hollywood types, and lived her own iconoclastic life. Katharine Hepburn told reporters whatever outrageous story entered her head and shut up one particularly nosy reporter in 1934 by telling him that yes, she had two children, and they were both black.[2]

Joan Crawford ran a contest in one movie magazine in which she rewarded fans who sent in the best pieces of acting advice to her. The constant support of the fans was obviously essential to the success of a movie star, and she, and the public relations department of her studio, used many different techniques to achieve and then to maintain her popularity. The best proof, of course, of the fans' loyalty was their attendance at all of the movies starring their favorite actress. Despite the critics, in the 1930s and 1940s, audiences followed the stars, whatever the plot or the quality of the movie. *New York Times* critic Mordaunt Hall lamented this fact in his review of Crawford's 1934 movie, *Sadie McKee*, when after panning the movie, he noted that Sadie "is acted by Joan Crawford which probably accounts for the throngs attracted to the Capitol yesterday."[3]

The movie stars of the 1930s generation came from a variety of class and family backgrounds. Katharine Hepburn, Rosalind Russell, and Elizabeth Taylor, for example, all came from upper-middle-class families; they were raised to believe in their own worth and to stand up for their own opinion. Hepburn and Russell, especially, had fathers who encouraged them as did

their mothers. Hepburn spoke admiringly of her mother, who was a suf-
fragist and birth control advocate, and her father, who was a physician;
both parents contributed to her sense of self assurance. "Good Lord," she
once said,

one of my earliest recollections is my mother making speeches, and raising hell—
a real suffragette, and in those days, that wasn't an easy thing to be—about 90
percent of the people in America—men and women—were against you if you were
a suffragette—made fun of you—she didn't give a damn—it was something she
believed in. Now with Dad trying to make a living as a doctor, of course it could've
got in his way professionally but they talked it over—decided people have to do
what they feel—it wasn't only the vote that was the issue.[4]

Hepburn's image, in all interviews, was that of a self-confident person,
someone who would succeed in whatever profession she chose. In 1950 she
told a reporter, "I have to be a person, not a piece in a pattern."[5]

Rosalind Russell's father was a lawyer, and her mother was an editor at
Vogue magazine. She recalled how her loud voice annoyed her mother at
the dinner table, while her father assured her that, since she wanted to be
heard, it was a useful instrument. She took her father's advice and always
projected her voice well beyond the third row of the theater. Russell considered herself a tomboy who played football and pool, knew how to fix
a carburetor, and learned at the age of six, she later said, that "males are
not as hot stuff and as omnipotent as they think they are."[6] Strongly influenced by both her parents, she continuously exhibited high spirits. *American*
magazine complimented her in 1941 by saying that her distinctive quality
was that "she dared to be herself."

Elizabeth Taylor arrived in Hollywood from England at the age of seven
and went from being a child star to adult star successfully. She has observed
how schooling at MGM, a traumatic experience for many child stars,
amused her. Even the formidable head of the studio, Louis B. Mayer, failed
to intimidate her. Taylor's family provided her with emotional support.
Biographer Dick Sheppard defined her strength and endurance as based on
four things: "a sound family foundation and a consequent inner assurance
which has never failed her; the mutual love and devotion of those closest
to her; a bond with the public which transitory crises could never sever;
and a professional knowledge of the crafts of film acting second to none."[7]

Though her mother had some of the characteristics of a pushy stage
mother, she also acted as a refuge for Taylor. In 1950, at the age of 17,
Elizabeth Taylor told interviewers that she was a traditional girl and very
concerned with her mother's opinion of her. "I'm being painted as a good-
time girl," she told Louella Parsons, "who stays out all hours of the night.
That is hard to take. If you could see how my mother cries, you'd know
what I mean."[8] Observers of the child star noted how unambitious and

undemanding she was, in contrast to the all-consuming careerist, Margaret O'Brien. "No one," commented a Hollywood reporter in 1955, "can accuse Elizabeth Taylor of storming front offices, demanding, fretting or weeping over lost roles."[9]

During her long tenure in moviemaking, Taylor's face appeared on many movie magazine covers; after Greta Garbo and Joan Crawford, she was probably the most photographed female movie star. Her every move was recorded and she once complained that her life was on display like a young woman schoolteacher in a small town. In two separate interviews in the mid–1950s, she displayed insight into herself: "Instead of pointing out my faults, people always told me how good I was. I never learned responsibility."[10] She also noted: "All my life I've been riding on a pink cloud. Because I'm a movie star, no one has the courage to tell me that I'm wrong. I have been told I was great when I was awful. . . . I am the little princess for whom everything is done."[11]

Since the private and public lives of Elizabeth Taylor have always been exposed to public view, she had to develop public explanations while most people kept their mistakes, and their rationalizations, to themselves. Taylor's superstardom has demanded her to be on public display, a pose that made self-analysis and honest assessment difficult. Within this context, her adaptability, vitality, and resilience enabled her to face pain, the death of loved ones, and loves lost. Her personal life has been more incredible and difficult than any script she played. In 1987, at the age of 55, she is both a grandmother and actress whose daily activities are still followed by the media.

Many actresses described in movie magazines came from one-parent families where the mother became the positive model of independence for the daughter to emulate. Bette Davis's parents, for example, divorced when she was eight years old, an unusual phenomenon in 1916. Her mother, Ruthie, had to earn a living to support Bette and her younger sister, Bobbie. Attorney Mr. Davis failed to support his family. Thus, Bette Davis saw a mother work at various jobs until she learned photography and became moderately successful at it. In high school, Davis decided to become an actress and after graduating spent some time at the Robert Milton–John Murray Anderson School of the Theater in New York. By 1930, at the age of 22, she was on her way to Hollywood under contract to Universal Studios. Once in Hollywood, the path was stormy but Davis's determination kept her going.

Silent stars Mary Pickford, Blanche Sweet, Mae Marsh, and the Gish sisters were all raised by mothers alone. Pickford's father was killed in an accident when she was five, Marsh's father died when she was four, the Gishs' father deserted the family when they were four and five, and Sweet's father deserted them when she was one; her mother died a year later and she was raised by a grandmother. Pickford's mother always played an active role in furthering her daughter's career. When Mary Pickford formed her own corporation and became its president, her mother became all the vice-presidents. Since the age of seven, Mary Pickford was the family bread-winner. She may have portrayed sweet juveniles until she was in her thirties, but in her private life she was an astute businesswoman.

Carole Lombard, Joan Crawford, Judy Holliday, and Doris Day are more examples of movie stars raised by divorced mothers. Lombard was a Hollywood favorite, an attractive blond with an impish smile. She was known as a notorious practical joker and an inventive curser. Her secret, and later not so secret, love affair with the king of Hollywood, Clark Gable, made her a favorite of the fan magazines. "Will Lombard's Marriage End Her Career?" asked a reporter of *Motion Picture* in 1939, just after her marriage to Gable. Would she give up her successful movie career for wifehood and motherhood? Readers bought the magazine eager to discover the answer to that important question. Would she give up the career she loved for the man she loved? The answer finally came toward the end of the article: yes, she would, for as the reporter editorialized, "underneath that trick Carole, you see, there has always been a real woman." Ostensibly, actresses and independent women are not real. The writer further revealed that Lombard confessed to her intimates that she hoped that Gable would ask her to give up her career for him. "I'd just like to let 'Pa' be the star, while I stay home and mend socks and mind babies."[12]

The childhood of Joan Crawford was unusually difficult. Her father disappeared when she was a baby, and her mother married a vaudevillian; the family moved to Oklahoma where they lived for six years when another disruption occurred. Her mother divorced her stepfather and married for a third time, now moving the family to Kansas City. By 1920, at the age of 12, Joan Crawford (whose real names were Lucille LeSueur, then Billie Cassin, and then back to Lucille LeSueur) was an awkward, insecure, overweight girl. She began dancing at 15 in an effort to overcome her shyness and to embark on a career of her own. The story sounds like a Hollywood movie: Crawford won an amateur dance contest, moved to Chicago, and then Detroit where a Shubert recruiter saw her and offered her a job in the chorus line of a Broadway musical. A contract with MGM in 1925 began her movie career.

Judy Holliday's parents separated when she was six in 1928, and Doris Day's parents divorced when she was twelve. In all of these cases, the women stars were raised by mothers alone, and the model for adult womanhood was that of a woman supporting her family. All of these young women grew up with a decisive, self-determining mother. They learned courage from their mothers; none had been actresses but all had been, often through necessity, autonomous women. They all encouraged their daughters to cultivate their unique talents.

Surely, most daughters of stable families, such as Hepburn and Russell's, do not achieve movie stardom, nor do they become independent women. Most girls from divorced families do not go on to Hollywood stardom. The family pattern of both parents encouraging their daughters toward self-development, though, provided the congenial atmosphere for female strength. Further, the model of a working mother who had to struggle to maintain her family left an indelible impression upon sensitive young women. The ingredient that most women movie stars shared was that of self-confidence, which was bred in childhood by supportive parents or a supportive mother. Rosalind Russell's father told her that a quitter never wins and a winner never quits, and she never forgot that message. Bette Davis admired her mother's uncomplaining willingness to work hard for the education and future of her daughters. Fan magazine readers recognized the spirit within these women as distinguishing them from others, but they also could derive strength and encouragement from that knowledge.

The biography of Barbara Stanwyck dramatically illustrated the importance of personality in determining outcomes. Born in Brooklyn in 1907, Stanwyck was orphaned at four. Being the youngest of five children, she was raised by an older sister. After finishing elementary school, she worked as a bundle wrapper, telephone operator, file clerk, and pattern cutter. She became a dancer and at the age of 16 toured with the Ziegfeld Follies. While dancing in an Atlantic City nightclub, she received a small part in a Broadway play and in 1927 was on her way to Hollywood. Throughout the 1930s and 1940s, she made innumerable movies, becoming one of the most popular and best paid actresses in the business. Early in her career, she demonstrated an iron will that was also evident in her screen portrayals.

She told one magazine writer how she dealt with wily Hollywood producers who reneged on promises:

I originally came to Hollywood with a written contract and a verbal understanding that I would be paid more money if I proved popular with movie fans. For many years I had such verbal agreements with New York stage producers, and I never experienced difficulty.

But when my motion pictures were successful and I reminded my employers of my verbal agreement, I was told that "I had a contract and must live up to it." I answered by keeping quiet until I was needed for a picture, then refusing to do that picture. I won the subsequent court fight and my salary was raised.[13]

One of Stanwyck's favorite quotations was, "It isn't life that matters, it's the courage you bring to it." Avid movie magazine readers had much to admire in her life story.

Those women who achieved stardom did so because their personalities and backgrounds combined to create determined, hard-working, ambitious women. In most descriptions of the major stars, mention is made of their unerring professionalism. Contrary to the popular myth of flighty, temperamental actresses, most were devoted to their profession. Joan Crawford was known as an extremely hard worker. Producer Jerry Wald was taken aback the first time he worked with her during the making of *Mildred Pierce*. He expected a difficult star, but instead he found that she was a person who "was on time every morning, who never complained how late we worked at night, who knew her lines and who was not only willing but positively humble about doing what she was told."[14]

Bette Davis rebelled only when she hated the innocuous parts she was forced to take under her long-term contract to Warner Brothers. While playing in a role she loved, she was demanding of herself, very serious, and totally committed to the venture. Similarly, Hepburn was known for her expertise on the set; she knew everyone's lines as well as the cameraman's angles, the director's perspective, and the best lighting for herself. Carole Lombard was equally knowledgeable on the set and enjoyed the mechanics of filmmaking. Elizabeth Taylor's seriousness on the set was also mentioned by her coworkers. Magazine articles shared these facts with their audience and, in so doing, helped to create the image of these movie stars as independent women, separate from the roles they played on the screen.

One question frequently asked and answered in the movie magazines was how the actresses managed their personal lives and their careers simultaneously. In 1945 Bette Davis wrote an article on this topic for *Motion Picture* magazine. She told her fans that her advice was specifically directed to women who had worked during the war for the first time and had no specific career or job; her remarks did not apply to women who had combined career and marriage simultaneously.

I am talking here only to those war-working wives who plan to continue working after their GI husbands come home from the war—women who never have tried the experience of combining a career and homemaking, but who are intrigued now with the idea, women who have found a business life stimulating and exciting as well as financially productive, yet know nothing of the problems, obligations and threats it will involve when combined with homemaking.

She advised such women to consider the prospect seriously. "You always can quit a job, but you cannot always recapture a marriage!"[15]

Within her discussion, however, Davis spoke out firmly against the general male domination of women: "Have you observed that the talk is always about what women should or should not do, never about what men should be prepared to face or accept?" Though outspoken, Bette Davis still acknowledged the separate spheres for the sexes when she proclaimed, "No husband should be expected to come home from his own full day's work to run a vacuum sweeper or clean up the kitchen."[16] Davis alternated between sharp criticisms of the male view of woman's place and pleasing platitudes describing the importance of domesticity. In good feminist tones, she criticized the cultural imperatives that kept women in the home as grim houseworkers, but then she relented by reminding her readers that "the wife with a job must not allow or want her husband to think of her, or treat her, like another man in business. She must be a wife, first, last and always, as far as he is concerned. Otherwise, she is an idiot and deserves to lose him."[17]

A woman must never put her work before her home, reminded professional actress Davis; yet earlier in the interview, she had asserted that "the accident of sex had nothng to do with human rights and justice in an enlightened world." Bette Davis exhibited great ambivalence on this sensitive and difficult subject. Proclaiming women to be human with equal rights to men was followed by utterances like: "She must be prepared to give her free time to the wants and pleasures of her children and husband, regardless of how exhausted she may be from her day's labors." She concluded by saying: "For no matter how great a career and success, without a home a woman cannot be happy. But I still say she *can* have both!"[18]

Rich contradictions characterized Davis's views. While raising a question that interested the unprecedented number of working women during World War II, she wavered between advocating independence for women while upholding traditional roles. She distinguished between career women, whose right to work went unquestioned, and the larger number of temporary workers who had entered the work force during the national emergency. But her priorities were clear: marriage, and its preservation, was more important for all women than work. Presumably, even career women should give up their careers if their marriages were in jeopardy. Her hopeful ending that a woman could have both was simply that: wishful thinking. Ideally, Davis argued, women were equal to men and were entitled to equal rights. Realistically, though, happiness for women only appeared in the form of marriage. Thus, without prescribing extensive cultural change, she merely hoped that with understanding, good will, and communication women could achieve success in both their personal and professional lives. What would happen if all working women enjoyed the new economic, psychological, and social freedom gained from working and wanted to keep it? Neither Davis nor most of the society's pundits could answer that question.

Journalists have gleaned one message from the many marriages of the stars, while contemporary feminists could develop a far different interpretation. Pop culture reporters have always described the private lives of entertainers as exotic and sensuous, but unnatural. Stars, being exceptional people, lived different lives from the masses, an expected phenomenon, but to insure admiration and prevent resentment, fans were treated to descriptions of the multiple problems resulting from fame and fortune. Fan magazine writers gave endless details of the unhappy marriages of the stars, of their alienated children, and of their fears. Consciously or unconsciously the preservers of the status quo insured loyalty to monogamy and family with these pictures of the movie stars' failed marriages.

From a feminist perspective, the frequent marriages of the stars could suggest a healthy desire to remain happy, to feel deserving of happiness; rather than be a martyr or self-sacrificer, female stars assertively ended bad relationships and sought new ones. Being financially more independent than most women, they did not have to endure unhappy marriages. They strove for private and public success. Accompanying their movie popularity, Davis, Crawford, and Taylor sought private happiness as well. Being products of the culture, they legitimized their love affairs by marrying. Unknowingly, perhaps, they were a new social type of woman, a married woman professional with a demanding public life. Unwittingly, they were the vanguards of the contemporary women's movement. They pioneered the wish for female self-identity. They were public independent women as well as Eves with the desires of Mary.

Bette Davis has been one of the most self-conscious and thoughtful writers on the tortuous problems of being a woman professional/wife-mother. Her autobiography, *The Lonely Life*, was so titled because, she said, she knew that ultimately she would spend her old age alone. However, she would not have done it differently. Married four times, widowed once, and divorced three times, she commented:

When a woman is independent financially and eclipses her husband professionally, the man suddenly finds it necessary to be a nineteenth century lord and master. He falls back on symbols that are insupportable to the self supporting wife. My mistake was to attempt the duality. I couldn't be both husband and wife and I tried.[19]

Davis, a thoroughgoing careerist, never dreamed of abandoning her career. Yet she wanted, as most women did, a husband and children. When she became a mother for the first time at age 39, she rejoiced and told Hedda Hopper:

You know Hedda, I've wanted Barbara for so many years I can't tell you. I used to think it was awful I hadn't had her when I was twenty-one. But now I realize how perfect it is to have her at my age. When I was a youngster, I was struggling so hard to get somewhere, now I've got the time to enjoy her.[20]

She told Rex Reed:

If I had to do it all again, the only thing I'd change is that I would never get married. But then I wouldn't have my kids and without them I would die. But my biggest problem all my life was men. I never met one yet who could compete with the image the public made out of Bette Davis.[21]

Davis never complained about her fate but rather analyzed her status cooly. The only dated comment, made in 1969, was her view that without marriage she could not have children, a position no longer held by all actresses or women in general. Bette Davis tried, in the 1930s, 1940s, and 1950s, to combine the best adult roles of both sexes. She failed, not because of a personal problem so much as a disharmony between the sexes. A career woman was a new type, while husbands still operated within old expectations about wives.

At the beginning of her fourth marriage, to actor Gary Merrill, she displayed her realistic, though hopeful, attitude toward marriage, when she told a reporter: "Now, really. I'm too old for romance stories. That's kid stuff. Let's just say I am wonderfully happy. I feel that this is a good marriage."[22] She and Merrill remained married for ten years, Davis's longest marriage; they adopted two children. But as she predicted in her autobiography, she is spending her old age alone.

Joan Crawford, who was married four times (widowed once and divorced three times), frequently discussed her personal life with magazine interviewers. She too sought the harmonic blend between personal and public success. Her first marriage to Douglas Fairbanks Jr. received a lot of publicity as he was the son of one of Hollywood's favorite leading men; second husband Franchot Tone introduced Crawford to the literary classics she had missed as a child. The progress and troubles of these two marriages were covered extensively in the movie magazines. She adopted a child with third husband Philip Terry; when that three-year marriage ended, she told Louella Parsons:

I can't say I'll never marry again, Louella, because—I get too lonely. I love my children, little Christina and Christopher, but I am a woman who does not like to be alone. Perhaps, "she smiled," I'll marry an Oscar who can't talk back. But seriously, "she went on," when and if I marry again, I want a man who will say, "We are not going to live in your house. I will give you a house, and you can have it any way you want, but it will be our home, not yours."[23]

Her fourth husband, Pepsi-Cola chief Alfred Steele, seemed to suit her; their four-year marriage ended only with his death in 1959. Crawford never married again.

Neither Davis nor Crawford fell apart due to their personal troubles. They did not become paralyzed or retreat into solitude. Their work provided comfort, security, and useful occupation. Acting gave them continual confirmation of their worth. They were independent personalities who shared the culture's values to the extent that they too wanted home, family, and husband, but they differed radically from most women in having another rich, demanding, and rewarding dimension to their lives.

Another good example of an actress who truly valued the traditional womanly roles, and lost them, yet survived, was Barbara Stanwyck. While married to her first husband, Frank Fay, she told an interviewer that

I would rather be Mrs. Frank Fay than anything else. I don't care what people say or think. Frank and I understand each other. I want two children, a little boy with red hair like Frank's and a little girl. What do a lot of pictures matter in the face of that?[24]

So Barbara Stanwyck raised her asking price for a movie to an unreasonable sum hoping to be denied work. But it did not turn out that way. Picture offers kept coming in for her while the demand for Fay waned. While making a movie, however, Stanwyck displayed her devotedness to home and husband by leaving the studio promptly at 5:30 P.M. The director might be driven to distraction "all because Frank likes an early dinner and she wanted to be home in time to eat with him."[25]

Stanwyck had had a difficult childhood, arriving in Hollywood after having seen the grimy underside of life. Fay had encouraged her to take the movie offers, but she never liked the atmosphere in Hollywood. Her marriage to Fay ended after seven years, and the experience changed Stanwyck's views on the subject. She concluded that she had submerged herself so totally in that marriage that she had lost herself. In a 1937 interview, she said:

I know what it is to have no life of my own at all. Even in little, inconsequential things. . . . You lose your life for love, this kind of love, though you are living. And this is what I'd advise girls not to do, to try not to do. . . . I know that I have reached the stage where I wouldn't place my whole trust in any man. Not unreservedly. This is no aspersion on the male sex or any member of it. I just don't think it's in them. I do trust women. I really believe that women are capable of disinterested friendship, of undivided loyalty, of keeping faith. . . .[26]

Stanwyck's second and last marriage to romantic idol Robert Taylor lasted from 1939 to 1951. Taylor left her for a younger woman and by most accounts hurt her very much. Stanwyck's work, however, occupied her mind and time. After movies no longer provided good parts for her, she turned to television and acted successfully for a number of years in the series "The Big Valley." Reading, donating her time to charitable endeavors, and sports continue to occupy her energies. Readers of the many articles on Stanwyck surely admired her quiet strength.

Katharine Hepburn, at 78 years old, remained active professionally until very recently. During her celebrated television interview with Dick Cavett, she claimed that a professional actress could not, and should not, marry as she could not devote adequate time to a husband and family. She never discussed her eight-year marriage to Ludlow Ogden Smith in the late 1920s nor her long-standing relationship with Spencer Tracy. She chose the image of independent woman, both on and off the screen. Hepburn seems to believe fervently in the scrupulous separation of social roles for women: a woman professional cannot be a wife and mother and vice versa. Hepburn, however, always the most reticent of the successful movie personalities, granted few interviews, and has maintained her silence on her personal life.

Elizabeth Taylor sought to combine personal and professional happiness in her busy life. She has borne three children, been married seven times (twice to actor Richard Burton), widowed once, and survived high-risk surgery. She has won the Academy Award twice, been much photographed, and starred in over 50 movies in a 40-year career. Like the generation of stars before her, Taylor survived the difficult world of moviemaking and discussed her life and her troubles in endless articles. She still is photographed regularly and has appeared several times on the cover of *People* magazine so that the under-40 generations also recognize her face.

Hepburn, Davis, and Stanwyck, particularly, offered their fans advice that would appeal to young women today. Because their lives as popular, successful women gave them unique opportunities, they appreciated the difficulty in achieving personal and professional success. Being movie stars, they led extraordinary lives, but their dreams and goals were culturally ordinary and predictable. Perhaps their studios and their fans would reject them if they suggested feminist or other radical solutions to the dilemma. So they counseled women to be independent while upholding traditional values of love, marriage, and family. They never suggested a serious reeducation program for men and women so that both sexes could escape traditional sex role definitions. *Motion Picture* surely would not publish such an outrageous suggestion.

All of these actresses provided readers with diverse modes of adaptation: the self-confident woman whose sense of self and pride in accomplishment enabled her to cope with personal unhappiness (Stanwyck); the successful female careerist who combined career with marriage (Russell); the much-married movie star whose career gave her enormous satisfaction but whose personal life continued to perplex her (Crawford); and the consummate actress who scrupulously supervised her career and her private life (Hepburn). Collectively, these movie stars provided large numbers of people with hours of entertainment, fantasy, and thoughtful considerations of women's lives in the United States.

Other evidence of the stars' impact can be gleaned from public opinion polls. Theater owners as well as studios were very interested in knowing who audiences liked. The *Motion Picture Herald* Fame Poll showed that, during the 1930s and 1940s, Joan Crawford and Bette Davis were each voted among the ten "best money-making stars." Crawford dominated the 1930s, having been in the top ten for five consecutive years: 1932–36, while Davis appeared in the poll in 1939, 1940, 1941, and 1944. According to

Internal Revenue Service figures, Barbara Stanwyck, with a $400,000 salary, was the highest woman wage earner in 1944, followed by Bette Davis.

In the area of awards, which demonstrates how the profession regarded the star, none rivaled Katharine Hepburn. She won the Oscar for Best Actress of the Year on four occasions, the only person in academy history to do so. The first was secured in 1933 for the ingenue role in *Morning Glory*. The next occurred 34 years later, in 1967, for *Guess Who's Coming to Dinner*, followed in 1968 by the award for *The Lion in Winter*. In 1981 she won an Oscar for *On Golden Pond*. Hepburn's movie career, in dramatic contrast to the other actresses discussed, enjoyed a renaissance in the late 1960s and 1970s, thereby introducing her to a new generation of movie-goers. In 1973 the winner of the Miss America contest declared that Katharine Hepburn was her heroine. With the women's liberation movement blossoming at that time, Hepburn represented a veteran fighter in the struggle for women's rights. Her independent women films gained a new audience on television, cable, and the new world of videotape.

Bette Davis follows in Academy Awards: she won one in 1935 for *Dangerous* and another in 1938 for *Jezebel*. Only five other actresses have won two or more Oscars in academy history. Davis was nominated ten times as was Hepburn. In 1950, Davis won the New York Film Critics Award for *All About Eve*. Her importance in the industry was well known; during the 1930s and 1940s, she was called the fifth Warner Brother because of her powerful role at the studio. Jack Warner declared that she was his favorite star.

Joan Crawford won one Oscar for her 1945 *Mildred Pierce*. She too had been nominated previously. Stanwyck had four nominations but never won; her stellar performance in *Stella Dallas (1937), The Lady Eve* (1941), *Double Indemnity* (1944), and *Sorry, Wrong Number* (1948) lost out in the balloting. However, her high earnings, as well as her large number of film credits, testified to her popularity. Rosalind Russell was nominated twice for *My Sister Eileen* (1942) and *Mourning Becomes Electra* (1947) but never won either.

By sharing their problems with their fans, by publicly discussing their traditional aims and their unusual lives, which made them both like their audience and different, these stars forged a significant link between actress and audience. Perhaps unknowingly, they displayed how independent women had not created a solution to their multiple wants and needs any more than traditional women had. Surely, fans appreciated the fact that no one has it all; no woman, or at least only few, combine Mary, Eve, and independent woman characteristics successfully. The women movie stars of the 1930s and 1940s, though, lived lives of contradiction. They had opportunities, experiences, and joys unknown to the majority of women, but they remained captives of the same cultural myths as their fans. Bette Davis surely meant it when she told Hedda Hopper how happy she was to become a mother at 39. And the much-married Elizabeth Taylor confessed in the 1980s that she has to marry the men with whom she sleeps.

Despite the feminist awareness of the 1980s, the current generation of women movie stars still struggle with the same issues. Female entertainers act out in public the same tensions and multiple demands and goals that all other women do; they share the same personal and cultural dreams. While displaying greater sexual freedom, in the permissive 1980s, they too generally operate within the boundaries of marriage and family. Meryl Streep, Sissy Spacek, and Sally Field, for example, have married and had children, while Jessica Lange and Farrah Fawcett live monogamously with lover and children. Marriage, motherhood, and personal career remain goals for women stars. Thus, the contemporary group joins with their predecessors who remain vibrant role models for all women seeking to define themselves in both an independent and traditional mode.

NOTES

1. Pam Payne, "Clubbing a Healthy Habit That'd Be Hard to Break," *Soap Box*, August 1977, pp. 3–4.

2. Beatrice MacDonald, "The career of an ugly duckling," *Modern Screen*, April 1934, pp. 68–69.

3. *New York Times*, May 19, 1934, p. 18.

4. Garson Kanin, *Tracy and Hepburn: An Intimate Memoir* (New York: Viking Press, 1971), p. 60.

5. Ann MacGregor, "Katie's Hep!" *Photoplay*, April 1950, p. 77.

6. Rosalind Russell, "The Kind of Gal I Am," *Saturday Evening Post*, September 29, 1962, p. 30.

7. Dick Sheppard, *Elizabeth* (New York: Warner Books, 1975), p. 17.

8. Louella O. Parsons, "Sub-deb or Siren?" *Photoplay*, March 1950, p. 76.

9. "Liz: Hollywood's Rarest Beauty," *Movieland*, April 1955, p. 30.

10. Ralph Edwards, "Queen Liz of Hollywood," *Photoplay*, December 1954, p. 102.

11. Gordon White, "Crying on the Inside?" *Motion Picture*, October 1955, p. 8.

12. "Will Carole Lombard's Marriage End Her Career?" *Motion Picture*, July 1939, p. 56.

13. James Fidler and Barbara Stanwyck, "Barbara Stanwyck Answers Twenty Timely Questions," *Movie Classic*, June 1933, p. 23.

14. Jerry Wald, "I Took One Look At Her," *Photoplay*, June 1947, p. 79.

15. Bette Davis as told to Kay Proctor, "Should Working Wives Quit After Victory?" *Motion Picture*, August 1945, pp. 36, 122–24.

16. Ibid., p. 122.

17. Ibid., p. 123.

18. Ibid., p. 124.

19. Bette Davis, *The Lonely Life* (New York: G. P. Putnam, 1962), p. 186.

20. Hedda Hopper, "Welcome Stranger!" *Modern Screen*, August 1947, p. 104.

21. Rex Reed, "Bette Davis," in his *Conversations in the Raw* (New York: New American Library, 1969), p. 17.

22. Liza Wilson, "That old magic," *Photoplay*, March 1951, p. 76.

23. Louella O. Parsons, "You're Welcome Joan," *Photoplay*, June 1946, p. 129.

24. Muriel Babcock, "Stanwyck, the Primitive," *Movie Mirror*, November 1931, p. 39.

25. Ibid.

26. Gladys Hall, "Barbara's Advice," *Radio Stars*, March 1937, pp. 102–3.

5

Bawdy Women Entertainers: From Burlesque to Pop Concert Halls

While independent women in film appear atypical in that medium, they become totally respectable and conventional when compared to the bawdy women entertainers of the past. Bawdy women spoke and sang of sexual themes and bathroom humor; they also made generally rude observations on forbidden subjects. These women performed before much smaller audiences in the confines of cabarets, nightclubs, burlesque houses, and vaudeville stages. Their presence in vaudeville required them to clean up their act for the family audience, but bawds such as Mae West and Sophie Tucker, though warned constantly by the stage managers about their outrageous behavior, ignored the admonitions and, for as long as they could, declared their freedom from restraint and good taste.

Bawdy women entertainers, by definition, represented a double insult to society: women, the delicate, conventional sex, exhibited outrageous behavior. Bawdy women overthrew two layers of cultural conditioning: that given to all cultural members and that reserved for the "fairer" sex. They took the Eve image and turned it around: no longer was woman's sexuality viewed as evil. Rather, to the bawdy woman performer, sexuality became a delightful, endlessly fascinating subject to discuss. Women could initiate sexual encounters, describe their conquests and failures, share their frustrations, and generally make fun of everyone who took the subject seriously.

They also displayed, as all iconoclasts do, a marked irreverence for sacred subjects. Nothing was out of bounds. No gesture, no thought, no action had to be self-censored or -controlled.

It has been the bawdy woman entertainer, the public displayer of shocking nonconformity, that implicitly stretched the boundaries of acceptability. After all, she shimmied in the prudish United States. She sang "I Don't Care" before adoring audiences. Whether it was Mae West, who shimmied, or Eva Tanguay, who made the "I Don't Care" song her trademark, bawdy women entertainers titillated and shocked twentieth century U.S. audiences. They were the left wing of popular women performers in a culture that defined women's roles and images carefully and conservatively. Their image was that of an independent Eve in its most extreme pose. The bawdy women walked a tightrope in their performances, usually falling to the side of disrepute.

The female rebel performer would not ever become a comfortable part of popular culture because she was too avant garde, too outrageous in her words and actions. Similarly, black women entertainers, many of whom also flourished as bawdy performers, never reached a large audience. They had the additional liability of being black; their performances were limited to black cabarets and nightclubs. In the next chapter, women comics, many of whom had the potential for bawdiness, will be discussed. Such television comics as Lucille Ball and Carol Burnett borrowed more from naughtiness than daring, though, and, therefore, were acceptable to the mainstream culture. If they had developed their comic spirit along bawdy lines, their careers would have been confined to night clubs. Joan Rivers, for example, controls her monologue when on television; in the clubs, she resembles the bawdy women entertainers of yesteryear.

In a time when burlesque represented the bawdy end of the popular cultural spectrum, women entertainers who were so inclined expressed their atypical and unconventional ideas and behavior on that stage. When the nightclub flourished, Sophie Tucker and Belle Barker could tell their risqué stories and sing their off-color songs in that intimate setting. In the 1960s and since, the rock concert stage attracted thousands of young people to a new forum for bawdiness. Janis Joplin and Bette Midler found their medium in these concerts. Historically, it was the adult, in the male-only setting of the burlesque house or the nightclub attended by couples, who attended bawdy performances. With the growth of the youth population, coupled with the explosion of rock n' roll in more and more extreme forms, 16 year olds were treated to rock stars shouting obscenities, gyrating their bodies across the stage, and discussing sexual activity in explicit terms.

Audiences generally have given their love and loyalty to both romantic heroines and bawdy women. Performances of both kinds of woman entertainer have attracted a large and steady following. Indeed, the audience, in its collective wisdom, has displayed its knowledge and understanding of human nature by accepting both images of women. The need for both freedom and limitation, for restriction and liberation, exists in everyone. And the women exalted in popular culture have captured both needs, both images. They have displayed both the conventional and the anarchic possibilities in human behavior; they have upheld and defied the female stereotype in our culture. Because they remain a minority in show business, they can provide their services while not offending society's sensibilities.

The unrestrained woman has more fun than the constrained, romantically determined heroine; she has a glamorous, often mysterious past, and she defies conventional expectations about women. Sometimes, in a paradoxical way, she too is bound by love, but during the course of the adventure, she appears free and unconventional. Some unconventional women escape conventional expectations. They remain free and in control. An Eva Tanguay, a Sophie Tucker, a Mae West, and a Bette Midler remained, and remain, friendly mockers of the romantic tradition, women outside the majority, rebels who move in and out of society.

Just as movie stars and their screen roles, and writers and their stories, are natural equations, so live performers and their performances go hand in hand. However, it is more difficult to document and reproduce live performances. There are firsthand and secondhand accounts of the acts, but they are partial, impressionistic, and highly selective. The researcher of bawdy women entertainers has the added problem of finding printed descriptions of off-color material, which are difficult to uncover. Further, the lines between the person and her persona blur more for live performers. Mae West acted on and off the stage and kept up the appearance of a constant satirist. The image created merged with the real-life personality more fully in the minds of the audience. It is harder to separate the two dimensions. Readers of popular magazines and newspapers generally were not introduced to the burlesque queens of the United States, with the exception of the well-publicized Eva Tanguay, Mae West, and Sophie Tucker.

No one was a more audacious practitioner of this entertainment style than Eva Tanguay (1878–1947). Calling herself the Queen of Vaudeville, Tanguay electrified audiences. Her greatest years, 1904–15, brought her fame and wealth. While working men earned $2 for a ten-hour day, Tanguay received $3,500 a performance. She was the "I Don't Care Girl," the title of one of her most popular songs. She wiggled, moved frenetically across the stage (one account said she covered the equivalent of 3.5 miles a performance), shook her wild hair, and sang in a high-pitched voice. She was the first to admit that she had little talent but an enormous capacity for self-promotion and outrageous behavior. One observer noted, "The mass of frizzy blond hair, animated arms and legs, and a big voice singing lyrics that no one would believe could be produced by a sane person was vaudeville's newest hit."[1] Mae West, an admirer of hers and an inimitable practitioner of the same art, said of Tanguay, "There are two kinds of headliners in vaudeville—the kind that draws and the kind that makes good, with occasionally a combination of the two, like Eva Tanguay, who does both."[2]

Tanguay was born in Marbleton, Quebec, of French Canadian parents. She had two brothers and a sister. The family moved to Holyoke, Massachusetts, when she was a child. At the age of eight, Tanguay acted in stage productions. She began as Little Lord Fauntleroy and went on to do musicals. In 1903 she became a headliner in *The Office Boy* and *The Chaperones*. In a musical comedy called *The Blond in Black*, she played a character called "The Sambo Girl." She so distinguished herself by her blackface performance of the role that the show was renamed *The Sambo Girl* and her part was enlarged. It was, however, on the vaudeville stage that she shone. She was billed as a singing comedienne, and as one commentator noted, "It is easy to analyze her act: it was assault and battery."[3]

Tanguay understood the value of publicity; she also appreciated the fact that the more audacious she became, the more attention she received. She loved writing and singing limericks to explain her fame: "When I put on tights/My name went up in lights!" she exclaimed, and in 1915 she sang: "There's method in my madness/There is a meaning for my style/The more they raise my salary, the crazier I'll be."[4] Many of the critics, however, were puzzled by her enormous success. Ada Patterson, a top woman reporter for the Hearst newspapers, wrote of a Tanguay performance:

Everyone is filled with breathless intensity. . . . Here she comes with quick fluttering steps and restless, outstretched hands, a dynamic personality of nerves and excitement . . . a trim, alert figure, held so tense and straight that energy exudes from it . . . a wild mop of stiff, tousled blond hair which seems charged with electric vigor . . . saucy, broad, good-humored face . . . large, smiling mouth and pertly turned-up nose . . . her small, impudent eyes. Every inch of her is alive. . . .[5]

In 1918 journalist Heywood Broun in the *New York Herald Tribune* criticized her for singing the "Marseillaise" in French, lambasting her performance as being vulgar and grotesque. He stated: "The only cheerful song in her repertory yesterday was one in which she hinted that some day she would retire. Miss Tanguay is billed as a 'bombshell.' Would be to Heaven she were, for a bomb is something which is carried to great height and then dropped."[6] Tanguay responded to the criticism by Broun by taking out a full-page advertisement in *Variety* in which she said:

Have you ever noticed when a woman succeeds how they attack her until her character bleeds? They snap at her heels like mongrels unfed, just because she has escaped being dropped into FAILURE'S biggest web. They don't give her credit for talent or art. They don't discount a very hard start. They don't give her credit for heartaches or pains; how she grimly held tight to the reins when the road ahead was rocky and dreary; how smiling she made every discouraging sneer. . . .[7]

Her spunk and aggressive pride rose from the page. Indeed, Tanguay had a very high opinion of her self-promoting abilities and credited her success to her style and her four press agents. She spoke frankly on the subject: "That's all there is to it. As a matter of fact, I am not beautiful, I can't sing, and I don't know how to dance. I am not even graceful."[8] But she stood her ground and continued to publicize her appearance on street corners. In one positive review of her act in the *Dramatic Mirror* of 1915, the reviewer declared, "If ever the United States becomes involved in war, we recommend Miss Tanguay as recruiting sergeant extraordinary."[9]

Tanguay's songs openly proclaimed her views. Besides "I Don't Care," she sang "I Love To Be Crazy," "I Want Some One To Go Wild With Me," "It's All Been Done Before but Not the Way I Do It," and "Go As Far As You Like." In 1908 she scandalized audiences with her Salome act in which her costume was described as "two-pearled." She later recalled how she performed the dance of the seven veils.

I was no classical dancer, so I mixed in some Highland Fling and Sailor's Hornpipe and everything else I knew. And I sang as I danced and dropped one veil after another. I also did something else that no one else had thought of. Instead of dancing around holding the papier mâché head I hired a Negro boy with big eyes. I sat him on the side of the stage, all covered up. As I began to dance, I uncovered his head, which, to the audience, appeared to be resting on a silver tray. As I moved about the stage his huge eyes also moved, following me.

The audience was electrified. But when the Mayor of New York heard about the dance, he sent word to put some clothes on or he'd close the show.[10]

An offer from Flo Ziegfeld prevented her from accepting the mayor's challenge, but Eva Tanguay continued to pack them in whenever and wherever she played. As late as 1922, she broke Loew's New York State Theater record with a $29,000 take at a top price of 50 cents.[11] Her tours around the country also resulted in headline stories. Tanguay had the reputation of being a brawler. She carried around $100 bills to give stagehands after she hit them for an alleged insult. In Evansville, Indiana, in 1905 she slept through the matinee performance and received a $100 fine from the manager. She retaliated during the evening performance by threading the stage curtain with a dagger. In 1914 in Sharon, Pennsylvania, at Morgan's Grand Theater, she berated the audience for being "hicks" and cursed the management because her dressing room mirror was not large enough. But people continued to come to her performances.[12] It was only when vaudeville died in the 1920s that Tanguay's career ended.

Eva Tanguay dominated vaudeville by all accounts. Her dubious talents for singing and dancing did not deter her. Brashness exuded from her every performance. She mocked society's view of women as demure and submissive and declared "I Don't Care What People Say." Her unconventionality was surely the basis for her allure; she magnetized her following with her direct, cheeky behavior, her wild appearance, and her suggestive lyrics. She was not alone in her day, but she was unique in her longevity on the vaudeville stage and her sustained popularity.

She had no immediate rivals, but two younger women achieved great fame as bawdy entertainers as well: Mae West and Sophie Tucker. West (1893–1980) was born in Brooklyn to prize fighter Jack West from whom, she claimed, she inherited her belligerence and toughness.[13] She sang and danced and played in many musical comedies and vaudeville revues. In 1912, while performing in Chicago, she saw black dancers do a dance they called the "shimmy shawobble." The dancers arched their bodies and moved in a sensual rhythm that appealed to West. The next night, in her encore, she introduced the shimmy to white audiences. She was 19 years old and ready to take on a respectable nation.

When she opened at the Model Theater in Philadelphia in 1912, the advertisement read: "She does a muscle dance in a sitting position. It is all in the way she does it, and her way is all her own."[14] Sime Silverman, Variety's founder and chief reporter in those days, reviewed her act and said, "She's one of the many freak persons on the vaudeville stage where freakishness often carries more weight than talent, but Miss West should be coached to deliver the full value of her personality." Silverman's definition of Mae West's fully developed personality and her own definition never quite meshed. In her next appearance, she wore a trick dress where the strap broke easily. When the manager reminded her that it was a family audience, she answered that she could not help it. The Variety reporter summed it up by saying, "The gal was always making a dress adjustment."[15]

Mae West continued on her self-chosen path. She seemed impervious to the criticisms as long as the audiences kept coming. Variety said in 1916 of her performance: "She'll have to clean up her style—she has a way of putting dirty meanings in innocent lyrics."[16] West later recalled that her manager was always warning her "that the Church would cause problems if she did not change her material."[17] The Keith-Albee vaudeville circuit, one of the largest in the business, was run by E. F. Albee who prided himself on being able to ferret out all examples of vulgarity. On being told that Mae West used bold material, he called her into his office for a private performance of the questionable song. As her accompanist at the time, Harry Richman, told the story:

She had a line in her 'Frankie and Johnny' number that went, "If you don't like my peaches, don't you shake my tree." She did this line as only Mae West could do it, and the men in the audience would scream and yell and go half-crazy.... When she did it for Albee, she clasped her hands close to one cheek and said it very clearly, almost childishly, and at the same time cast her eyes upward, the most mournful creature in the entire world. I nearly fell off my piano stool.[18]

Needless to say, Albee resumed her booking and wondered what the complaints were about.

In 1921 West brought down the house each night with her shimmy dance in a show called "Mimic World." But in the following year, she presented a new act to the Colonial Theater in New York and won Silverman's praise: "No dancing in the present act. It's clean as a whistle and good. It can play anywhere and will entertain anywhere. Harry Richman at the piano. The years Mae West wasted!"[19] Not only did West not consider the past years as wasted, but she began writing more unconventional material for her act. In 1926 she opened in New York in a play she wrote under the name of Jane Mast. It was called *Sex*. Bob Sisk, the *Variety* reviewer, called it "a nasty red-light district show."[20] A lot of people, he reported, left the theater after the first act. Even more left after the second. After a run of 11 months, the police suddenly closed *Sex*, and Mae West was charged with damaging the morals of her audience. She was sentenced to ten days in the Welfare Island workhouse after a well-publicized trial. West drove to the workhouse in her Rolls Royce amid cheering crowds. While there, she insisted upon wearing her own silk lingerie rather than the rough cotton nightdress. She was released after eight days, having received two days off her sentence for good behavior. She donated a thousand books to the prison library upon her exit.

Never deterred and always undaunted, Mae West opened in 1928 with her comedy *Pleasure Man*, a story about a stud who loves and leaves women. Included in the cast were female impersonators. In the final scene, while the stud is murdered by the husband of a jilted woman, the impersonators went through their routines. The *Variety* reporter saw the opening night performance. This was fortunate for posterity's sake as the show closed the next night. He reported:

It's the queerest show you've ever seen. All of the Queens are in it. . . . If that Mae West can't think of the oddest things. . . . The party scene is the payoff. If you see those hussies [actors playing homosexuals] being introduced to do their specialities, you'd pass out. . . . The host sang a couple of parodies, one going "When I Go Out and Look for the Moon." Now I ask you. Another guest very appropriately sang, "Balls, Parties and Banquets," and I ask you again. . . . Go early, for some of the lines can't last.[21]

The police closed the show down for its allegedly obscene content. West defended *Pleasure Man* and, after a very costly trial, won the case.

The comedic style of Mae West was based upon exaggerated physical gestures, making fun of sexuality, and throwing off witty one-liners. Typical of her witticisms were, "she's the kind of girl who climbed the ladder of success, wrong by wrong." "It is better to be looked over than over-looked." "Between two evils, I always pick the one I never tried before." "Too many girls follow the line of least resistance—but a good line is hard to resist."[22] In 1928 she also wrote and starred in a Broadway musical called *Diamond Lil*. West played the part of a dance hall owner who loved her diamonds and her men, who made fun of peoples' vanities, and who always got what she wanted. It was rewritten for the movies and became her successful *She Done Him Wrong*. Years later, she said of Diamond Lil, "I'm her and she's me and we're each other."

Mae West went on to a movie career and starred in ten movies between 1932 and 1943. Her "gaudy humor" as described by the *New York Times* film critic in his review of *She Done Him Wrong* amused audiences enormously, and the good performance of newcomer Cary Grant was overshadowed by her dominating presence.[23] The critics grew less and less amused, however, as her self-parody became more and more extreme. By 1940 the predictable entourage of admiring men, West's considerable girth, and her burlesque of sex seemed stale and overdone to some. Decades later, a new generation of moviegoers discovered West in the 1970 *Myra Breckinridge*.

Her appearance on the radio often resulted in public outcry. On the "Edgar Bergen-Charlie McCarthy Show" of December 12, 1937, for example, she performed a skit with actor Don Ameche in which they portrayed Adam and Eve before the Fall. West as Eve kept urging Adam to leave the Garden of Eden as she wanted to "expand her personality." Adam, on the other hand, was content to fish and enjoy the pleasures of the garden. Practical Adam reminded her that they had a lease on the place. "It's too safe," she responded. A woman needed excitement, trouble, and tension to keep her interested in life. Adam also told Eve that she was made from one of his ribs and, therefore, should be obedient. Her quick retort was "I'm the floatin' rib." In a later repartee, he declared that he was man number one and Eve replied: "But are you number one man?"

Eve then showed her temptress qualities by tricking him into eating the forbidden fruit and kissing him loudly. "That was the original kiss!" she declared. The Catholic Church quickly registered its disapproval, and arbiters of family entertainment insisted that she was unacceptable to middle-class sensibilities. Indeed, the increase in censorship on the radio and the movies of the 1930s severely limited her career.[24] With burlesque on the wane and vaudeville houses giving way to the movies, there were few outlets for her bawdy shows.

Sophie Tucker (1887–1966) came from an immigrant Jewish family that settled in Hartford, Connecticut, where her father operated a restaurant. The clientele was often composed of traveling entertainers, and Sophie helped out in the restaurant both as a waitress and a singer. The Yiddish actors who frequented it encouraged Sophie to go into show business, but while they had the Yiddish stage in mind, she thought about burlesque and vaudeville. In the fall of 1906, she left her baby (her husband had already left after a brief marriage) with her parents and moved to New York City.[25]

Tucker's career was very much in the "working herself up the hard way" tradition. She sang in a New York City club for $15 a week. Every night she mixed audience requests with prepared numbers. She later estimated that she performed between 50 and 100 songs every night. After singing at an amateur night event in one theater, she was hired to perform on the Park circuit. Entertainers "on the circuit" traveled to various towns in New England and performed at local theaters. Her agent advised her to blacken her face and sing in the then popular "coon style." Although she hated this approach, Tucker found that audiences enjoyed it. She was a very large woman, weighing over 175 pounds and possessing a husky voice to match her girth. By hiding her facial expression in blackface, she could exploit her appearance by singing romantic ballads mockingly.

Sophie Tucker was billed as the "Manipulator of Coon Melodies." In 1909, after she played briefly in the Ziegfeld Follies, she abandoned blackface forever. By that time she had developed her trademark style, which included songs sung with a Yiddish accent, risqué songs, and comic interludes. Like her predecessors, Tucker had trouble with the law. In Chicago she was once ordered by the police to stop singing "Angle Worm Wiggle."[26] She took the matter to court and lost. It is noteworthy that Tucker and West consistently fought censorship, and though self-interest was obviously the motive, they were lonely voices for freedom of speech in that period. Tucker, like West, was amply endowed and her wiggly accompaniment to a song, her suggestive asides, and her lewd gestures offended the arbiters of good taste. But everyone kept coming back for more, which gave the performers ample opportunity to contemplate the hypocrisy of the censors.

Composers Fred Fisher and Jack Yellen began writing her songs, many of which featured double entendres. Tucker became known as the "red hot mamma," a term taken from black singers denoting a sexy woman who is not afraid to talk about sex. "When They Start to Ration my Passion, It's Gonna Be Tough on Me" and "You Can't Serve Love in Dishes, and You Can't Sew a Button on a Heart" were two songs written by Yellen during this period. Her theme song, "Some of These Days," also became part of her repertory. Tucker performed at the newly emerging nightclubs in the 1920s; indeed, her greater successes were in nightclubs where the intimate atmosphere encouraged her risqué lyrics.[27]

Tucker did in nightclubs what Mae West and Eva Tanguay had done on the stage. She spoke directly about sex, made fun of prudishness, and proclaimed her sexual independence. "No One Man is Ever Going to Worry Me," "Make Him Say Please," "You've Got to See Your Mama Ev'ry Night," and also "No One Can Satisfy Any One Man All the Time," "I'm Living Alone and I Like It," and "It's Never Too Late" were songs typical of Tucker's message. She usually belted her songs but was capable of a quiet, demure delivery as well. Well corseted (again like West) and bejewelled, Sophie Tucker told men in her audience not to take themselves so seriously; she told women that life began at 40, which she was by 1927, and that the older you get, the better you get.

Sophie Tucker built up a large and faithful audience all over the country. She continued to sing into old age, never formally retiring. By the early 1960s, when she was in her seventies, nightclubs began closing as the older generation stayed home and younger fans attended rock concerts. But from the 1900s through the 1950s, Tucker entertained large audiences who laughed at her bawdy songs and cried at her sentimental ballads, such as "My Yiddishe Mama," which she sang in Yiddish and English.

In the 1960s, young people responded to the bawdiness of the few women who sang in the world of rock and roll. Janis Joplin (1943–70) combined the raucousness of black bawdy singers with the zaniness of Eva Tanguay and Mae West, and she did it in the new world of rock music. Born in Port Arthur, Texas, she was a rather unattractive young woman who, in high school, saw herself as an outsider wanting very much to be accepted. At the age of 19, she began singing in a nightclub in Beaumont, a town near Port Arthur. Observers immediately noted her raw, loud, and sensual style; some compared her to the black blues singers Bessie Smith and Billie Holiday, whom she admired, while others considered her loud, rakish style to be uniquely her own.[28]

In 1963 Joplin moved to San Francisco where she became involved in the Haight–Ashbury flower children culture of the period, took drugs, drank heavily, and sang in small clubs. She returned to Port Arthur in 1965 to recover from drug abuse but went back to San Francisco the following year, when she became part of a group called Big Brother and the Holding Company. In June 1967 she attracted considerable attention at the Monterey Pop Festival with her singing of Wille Mae Thornton's song "Love Is Like a Ball and Chain." After that, record offers began. On the three albums Joplin recorded, she sang of fickle men, of free women, and of mean women seeking happiness in this difficult world. "Down on Me," "Love Is Like a Ball and Chain," "Cry Baby," and "Little Piece of My Heart" were among her most popular songs. Joplin's live performances were emotional experiences. She drank Southern Comfort liqueur on the stage, screamed out her songs often until she became hoarse, and gyrated continuously. *Time* magazine called her concerts a "kind of cathartic theater of the young." Audiences identified with her cries for love, her acknowledgement of pain, and her admission of weakness. She died in 1970 at the age of 27 from a mixture of drugs and alcohol.

Rock commentator Ellen Willis compared Joplin's treatment of the blues song "Ball and Chain" with Thornton's original rendition. She believed that Thornton sang in a manner that "carefully balances defiance and resignation, toughness and vulnerability," while Joplin sang all-out, exposing her neediness and crying for the man to stay with her. Willis concluded: "To sing the blues is a way of transcending pain by confronting it with dignity. But Janis wanted nothing less than to scream it out of existence, to annihilate it with her voice, even if she had to annihilate herself in the process."[29] While a Big Mamma Thornton or a Bessie Smith preserved her integrity while singing of love lost, Joplin seemed to plead, whine, and cajole the man to stay with her. In a posthumous album called *Joplin in Concert*, she talked to the audience between songs: "See, you gotta, when you wanna hold somebody, you gotta hold him like it's the last minute of your life, baby. You gotta hold on, hold on, hold on."[30] Of all the bawdy women performers, she was the one who took herself seriously.

Bette Midler, who calls herself (among other things) "Trash with Flash," was born in Honolulu in 1945, the third daughter in a family of four children. Midler recalled her high school years this way: "I was not a hip color. I was white in an all Oriental school. Forget the fact that I was Jewish. They didn't know what that was. Neither did I. I thought it had something to do with boys."[31] Midler's irrepressible humor, her desire to show off, and her natural talent as a singer and performer motivated her to go to New York in 1965. She had small parts in the chorus of *Fiddler on the Roof* and then as Tevye's eldest daughter, Tzeitel. Following that experience, she got a job at the Continental Baths, a homosexual bathhouse with entertainment; it was there that she developed her famous persona: the Divine Miss M. She wore black lace corsets and gold lamé pedal pushers, sang old songs of the 1940s and 1950s, and acted outrageously. Midler cursed, told dirty jokes, discussed sex constantly, and made fun of everyone, including herself.

Stephen Ostrow, the owner of the baths, said that Midler's insecurities propelled her into grossly exaggerated behavior and provided her with the energy to succeed. Whatever the motive, it gave her the unique and bawdy style that became her. In her live performances that followed around the country, she constantly added new material to the skits and personas she had developed at the baths.[32] In a concert tour called "De Tour 82/83," one reporter described her performance in ways that were reminiscent of Eva Tanguay. Midler motored across the stage in a wheelchair dressed like a mermaid with her tail flapping behind. She portrayed actress Meryl Streep as Sophie (from the movie *Sophie's Choice*) as a Borscht Belt comedienne. "Through sheer force of personality," critic Don McLeese continued, "she makes her stylistic eclecticism into a personal affirmation. Selling herself rather than a song, she's a better entertainer than a vocal interpreter."[33]

Just as Eva Tanguay borrowed from the news of her day, so Bette Midler became a social commentator known for her irreverent tones. While singing of love, she mocked her female fans for their slavish devotion to men. In her 1987 movie, *Outrageous Fortune*, she tamed her bawdiness a bit but still displayed her openness about discussing sexual subjects. In sharp contrast to the character played by the proper Shelley Long, Midler swore profusely, initiated all kinds of crazy adventures, and bragged of her sexual conquests. In a 1987 interview with Barbara Walters, Midler claimed to have given up her bawdy and tacky persona, since she said, "everyone is tacky now; I think I'll be royalty."

Bette Midler consciously created the new selves she portrayed in her live performances and in the movies. She told Gloria Steinem: "Actually, I'm getting more disguises—and I'm proud of that. Basically, I'm an actor who's looking for characters to assume. I'm proud of the fact that I have new voices, new accents, new tricks, new characters."[34] Midler, then, cultivated the bad girl image because it clearly appealed to young audiences who, in their adolescence, sought heroes and heroines who upheld their rebellious view of society. Midler fit the bill.

In style and content, Bette Midler is in the noble bawdy tradition begun by Eva Tanguay and Mae West early in this century. No subject was sacred or beyond scrutiny to any of them. The woman's body, human sexuality, the family, love, and ambition were all worthy subjects for their biting satire. Midler, Tanguay, and West could take traditional love songs and sing them in such a way as to reveal new meanings and comic reactions. They seemed incapable of being shocked by any human action or reaction though they strove to shock their audiences. While Eva Tanguay admitted that her shock appeal raised box office receipts, both West and Midler, knowingly or unknowingly, probed society's views of women, romance, and sexual relations. Coincidentally, they both flourished in periods of women's reform: West during the suffrage era and the liberated 1920s, and Midler during the heyday of the women's liberation movement. Their routines captured the woman's ambivalence toward love and romance, the desire to be Eve while not appearing to be her. Their bawdiness was an essential part of their appeal; crowds followed Mae West to every court appearance she made.

The bawdy women entertainers openly affirmed what the traditional enemy had always proclaimed: women were Eves, sexual temptresses, active and aggressive in their pursuit of pleasure. Rather than deny or hide this view, these performers acknowledged and declared it proudly and boldly. They probably delighted some members of their female audiences who secretly agreed with their blunt posture and point of view. The bawdy women brought out into the open the forbidden subject, thus being labeled unconventional and unacceptable. But their actions encouraged new imaginings for women, other human possibilities. In the more liberated 1980s, the explicit sexual references of Bette Midler appear less shocking, but her rakish smile still suggests that she understands how enormously amusing it is to hide discussions of sex.

Bawdy women entertainers have appeared in every generation of this century. Ironically, however, just as pure romance has a harder time existing in the sexually permissible 1980s, so vulgarity, grossness, and bawdiness may also have a difficult time. The most extreme examples of uninhibited rock musicians seem to burn themselves out rather quickly, and the ability to shock young audiences diminishes since they greet every audacity with joy. Mae West, Sophie Tucker and their numerous black women counterparts proclaimed that women had sexual natures and were willing to discuss the subject, but the message is no longer shocking or new. The appearance of West's 1927 play *Sex* with homosexuals and transvestites on stage would no longer lead to the police closing the show down. Bawdiness may acquire a good name, even for women, in the congenial 1980s.

NOTES

1. Anthony Slide, *The Vaudevillians: A dictionary of vaudeville performers* (Westport, Conn.: Arlington House, 1981), pp. 146–48.

2. Quoted in John E. DiMeglio, *Vaudeville U.S.A.* (Bowling Green: Bowling Green University Press, 1973), p. 81.

3. Douglas Gilbert, *American Vaudeville: Its Life and Times* (New York: Dover, 1940).

4. Quoted in Charles Samuels and Louise Samuels, *Once Upon a Stage: The Merry World of Vaudeville* (New York: Dodd, Mead, 1974), p. 63, and Slide, *Vaudevillians*, pp. 1, 48.

5. Quoted in Samuels and Samuels, *Once Upon a Stage*, pp. 54–55.

6. Abel Green and Joe Laurie, Jr., *Show Biz: from vaude to video* (New York: Henry Holt, 1951), p. 171.

7. Allen Churchill, *The Great White Way: A Re-creation of Broadway's Golden Era of Theatrical Entertainment* (New York: E. P. Dutton, 1962), p. 209, and Green and Laurie, *Show Biz*, p. 192.

8. Quoted in Gilbert, *American Vaudeville*, p. 329.

9. Quoted in DeMeglio, *Vaudeville U.S.A.*, p. 81.

10. Samuels and Samuels, *Once Upon a Stage*, p. 64.

11. Green and Laurie, *Show Biz*, p. 277.

12. Ibid., p. 330.

13. Mae West lived long enough to write and revise her life story many times. Some good sources on her include Andrew Bergman, *We're in the Money* (New York: Harper and Row, 1971), Joseph Weintraub, *The Wit and Wisdom of Mae West* (New York: Avon Books, 1967), and Mae West, *Goodness Had Nothing to Do With It* (Englewood Cliffs, N.J.: Prentice Hall, 1959). An interesting background article on burlesque comedy is Jill Dolan, "What, No Beans? Images of Women and Sexuality in Burlesque Comedy," *Journal of Popular Culture* (Winter 1984): 37–47.

14. Green and Laurie, *Show Biz*, p. 26.

15. Ibid., p. 27.

16. Ibid., p. 169.

17. DiMeglio, *Vaudeville U.S.A.*, p. 50.

18. Quoted in ibid., p. 51.

19. Green and Laurie, *Show Biz*, p. 277.

20. Ibid., p. 288.

21. Ibid., p. 289.

22. Weintraub, *Wit and Wisdom*, pp. 38, 43, 51–52.

23. "She Done Him Wrong," *New York Times*, February 10, 1933, p. 12.

24. Original recording of the December 11, 1937, show and recounted in Fred MacDonald, *Don't Touch That Dial!: Radio Programming in American Life from 1920 to 1960* (Chicago: Nelson-Hall, 1979), p. 106.

25. Sophie Tucker's autobiography is *Some of These Days: The Autobiography of Sophie Tucker* (Garden City, N.Y.: Doubleday, Doran, 1945). An excellent secondary source on her life and career is in Lewis A. Erenberg, *Steppin' Out: New York Night Life and the Transformation of American Culture, 1890–1930* (Westport, Conn.: Greenwood Press, 1981).

26. DiMeglio, *Vaudeville U.S.A.*, p. 146.

27. Two popular records by Tucker that can give contemporary listeners insight into her lyrics and style are *Some of These Days* (Pelican Records LP133) and *Sophie Tucker: Cabaret Days* (Mercury Records MG 20046).

28. Myra Friedman's biography, *Buried Alive: The Biography of Janis Joplin* (New York: Bantam Books, 1973), is a good introduction to the subject.

29. Ellen Willis, *New Yorker*, August 14, 1971, p. 81.

30. Quoted in Richard Lupoff, "Janis Joplin: Death Watch," *Ramparts*, July 1972, p. 52.

31. Clair Safran, "Who Is Bette Midler and Why Are They Saying Those Terrible Things About Her?" *Redbook*, August 1975, p. 57.

32. Some of the many articles on Midler are: Warren Hoge, "Bette Midler Goes Hollywood," *New York Times Magazine*, December 10, 1978; Charles Michener, "Bette Midler," *Newsweek*, December 17, 1973; and Timothy White, "The Homecoming: Bette Midler Outgrows Her Hollywood Dreams in 'The Rose,' " *Rolling Stone*, December 13, 1979.

33. Don McLeese, "Bette Midler Connects with Her tour de force," *Chicago Sun-Times*, February 28, 1983, p. 37.

34. Gloria Steinem, "Our Best Bette," *Ms.*, December 1983, p. 44.

6

Women Comics: From Music Halls to Television

Marys, Eves and independent women can be comics. Women with the proper personality and angle of vision have been, and continue to be, effective practitioners of humor. They turned potential disaster into hilarity and shared, with their audience, laughs. But the comedy business, like all other aspects of show business, is bound by cultural rules and expectations. Among them is the belief that women should be ladylike, demure, and quiet. Women comics, like bawdy entertainers, defy the culture. They intentionally contort their faces, mess their hair, and utter derisive and self-deprecatory lines. By making fun of themselves, they cause their audiences to look and laugh at their own frailties. They question things and assault the barriers between polite and rude.

The type of comedy chosen by a woman depends upon the dominant image with which she identifies. Mary types might be nitwits or screwballs, while independent women would do physical comedy or satire. Eves are the bawdy comics already described. Because of the richness and diversity of comic possibilities, it is necessary to create some categories. For example, comics can be roughly divided between those who perform solo and those, much more numerous comics, who appear in situation comedies. This discussion will focus primarily upon the multiple types of women comics who operate within situation comedy. Though there are mutations and mergers of characteristics, the following types of women comics can be identified: nitwit/screwballs, domestic comics, physical comics, self-deprecators, and satirists.

The nitwit/screwball exploits an alleged female trait: that women are dimwitted and out of touch with reality. The dizzy blonde is a variant. The nitwit type has had a great many exemplars from silent film to radio to sound movies and television. Often, they are teamed with a helpful man who feeds them their lines and saves them from disaster, a clear example of the Mary image merging with its comic expression.

Domestic comics, perhaps the largest single group, operate within a family setting; they either see their situation as humorous and find humor in their family, or they are the butt of family jokes. Thus, they can be active or passive actors in the comedy.

Physical comics have pies thrown in their faces and, in turn, haul off and hit their opponents, slip on bananas, and throw buckets of water at people doing the same to them. They are the most unladylike women, willing to appear in frumpy clothes and look unattractive. Sometimes, this type also possesses nitwit/screwball features. Lucille Ball and Carol Burnett are good examples of this merged comic persona. Their willingness to make fun of themselves, to expose their weaknesses, while also displaying resilience and power qualifies them as independent women as well.

Self-deprecators demonstrate the strength that allows them to expose personal weaknesses in public. Valerie Harper as Rhoda on television in the 1970s constantly made fun of her insecurities and neuroses. Joan Rivers focused upon her seemingly inadequate figure in her routines. The self-deprecators also joked about the inadequacies of other people, but they bravely exposed their own vulnerabilities to public ridicule.

Satirists are probably the most sophisticated comedians as they comment on social practices and values. Their material demonstrates an understanding and knowledge of their culture that is more studied than the comics who rely on physical humor. The satirist can operate within a family situation, such as Bea Arthur as Maude in the 1970s television series, or she can create her own skit, her own social environment, as Fanny Brice did on the stage of the Ziegfeld Follies. The satirist is often a solo performer and is the rarest breed among women comics. The reasons seem to be culturally motivated; until recently, women were not trained or encouraged to offer commentary on social, political, or religious issues, either in serious or humorous form.

NITWITS/SCREWBALLS

Pretty blondes seemed to be susceptible to the nitwit variety of humor. Perhaps the unspoken assumption was that their concern for their appearance made them so narcissistic that they could not pay attention to anyone else. And what an effective way for society to punish them for their beauty!

Audiences gained an advantage over this appealing woman through laughter. Further, the nitwit image closely tied the woman to a childlike pose; she always needed an adult, in the form of the hero, to rescue her from her inattentions and errors. Another variation on the image allowed her to be far cannier than originally assumed. Her logic, her world view, ultimately redeemed her.

In silent film, Constance Talmadge (1899–1973) often played the nitwit. A beautiful blonde with an elegant face and figure, Talmadge's beauty was compromised by her dizzy and distracted persona. Sometimes she played the cute flirt whose seemingly innocent advances always got her into trouble before she was saved by the hero and taught the proper lesson. In the 1923 film *Dulcy*, for example, she made her husband's prospective client engage in rigorous exercise only discovering later that he hated athletic activity. Talmadge blended coquettishness with distractedness in her portrayals. She teased men but always acted as if there could never be any adverse consequences to her behavior.

In *Her Sister from Paris* (1925), she played a twin who forgot the fact that she was masquerading as her sister and got herself into ridiculous situations. In a role where she was a hapless bandit, *Venus of Venice* (1927), Talmadge entered a fashionable dining room in stolen clothes and sat down next to the woman whose clothes she was wearing. Talmadge's pretty face and absurd actions offered audiences the unexpected contrast that evoked laughter.

In an article she wrote for *Motion Picture* magazine in 1927, "The Tragedy of Being Funny," Talmadge stated that comedy is a very serious business requiring careful preparation and thought. "And in the comedies that I do, which might be called sophisticated stories of modern life, one can't just dash on and be funny. There are subtle shades of humor that have to be caught by the camera, which actually only captures fifty per cent of what the human eye takes in."[1] Talmadge characterized her humor as "refined clowning" and displayed a self-conciousness and articulate awareness of her actions. All human situations were potentially comic, and the art of the comedian was to exploit the humorous possibilities of the situation. In a sense, the article by Talmadge contradicted the nitwit pose she presented in film. One observer noted that "her enjoyment reserve has never been exhausted. Whatever she does, she loves."[2]

While Constance Talmadge had to display her silliness largely through facial gestures in silent film, sound movies and radio gave nitwit comics rich verbal opportunities. Perhaps the queen on radio was Gracie Allen (1906–64). Born in San Francisco to a family of vaudevillians, she left school at 14 and went into show business with her three sisters. In 1923 she met George Burns, whom she married three years later. They formed an act and toured the vaudeville circuit. Eddie Cantor brought them to radio in 1932, and the following year they got their own show, which became one of the best loved radio programs. They remained on the radio for 17 years and in 1950 moved to television. Gracie retired in 1958 and died six years later.

Gracie Allen was the queen of the nitwits, the ingenuous, sweet woman whose unpredictable responses to situations always left the audiences laughing. Her real-life and radio husband, George Burns, was her straight man. He fed her the opening lines that resulted in her illogical and unexpected witticisms. Gracie once said to George: "Why, if you don't believe me when I'm telling the truth, when I'm not telling the truth you might think I was lying." Many of the funny stories concerned Gracie's family who seemed to be as crazy and unpredictable as she was. In one routine, Gracie told George that she was going to send her brother Willie, who was joining the army, a yo-yo in case he went to Egypt. The following dialogue ensued:

George: I don't understand.

Gracie: Well, you know how lazy he is. He always wants to play with a yo-yo, but doesn't like to move it up and down.

George: I still don't understand.

Gracie: Well, they ride camels there, don't they? and they sway up and down all the time, so all he'll have to do. . . .

George: I get it, Gracie. Silly of me not to have figured it out for myself. What did you get him in case they send him to the Pacific islands?

Gracie: A knife and a hatchet.

George: In case he has to hack his way through the jungle?

Gracie: No, they grow bananas and coconuts there, don't they? Well, he likes banana splits with chopped nuts.

George: Say good night, Gracie.

Gracie: Good night.[3]

The wit of Gracie Allen depended upon preserving her naive persona. Her ingenuousness was supposed to be natural and childlike. Her fresh and unexpected version of reality often had its own logic as evidenced in this interchange between Gracie and Eddie Cantor on his 1931 radio show, the "Chase and Sanborn Hour." Cantor said he wanted to be the president of the United States.

Gracie: You can't be president of the United States. My father told me this morning that he is going to be the President of the United States.

Cantor: Your father?

Gracie: Yes. My father said, "Gracie, if you can get on the Chase and Sanborn Hour, then I'll be President of the United States."[4]

On another occasion, George asked Gracie: "Did you ever hear silence is golden?" Gracie replied: "No, what station are they on?"[5]

Gracie often confused the meaning of words, which led to a comic dialogue. When George complimented her and called her a wizard, she said: "I'm a wizard?" and George asked her if she knew the word's meaning. "Yes," she answered, "a snowstorm." This, of course, led to further puns on blizzard and lizard. George wondered whether something unusual had occurred to Gracie when she was a baby. Gracie had the last line, and the last laugh: "When I was born, I was so surprised I couldn't talk for a year and a half."[6]

A variation of the nitwit is the screwball, a form that flourished in the movies of the 1930s. No one was more clearly identified with this image than Carole Lombard. She was born in Fort Wayne, Indiana, in 1908 to an affluent family named Peters (her real name was Jane Alice Peters). Her parents divorced when she was seven, and her mother took Jane and her two older brothers to Los Angeles. When Jane was 11, silent movie director Alan Swan saw her boxing with her brother in the front yard and hired her for a picture called *The Perfect Crime*. Although she became quickly infected by the movie bug, she returned to junior high school. After she graduated, Jane began hanging around the film units of Mary Pickford and Charlie Chaplin, hoping to get a part in a movie. At the age of 15, she played a lead opposite Edmund Lowe in *Marriage in Transit*. A precocious teenager, she astonished veterans with her ability to ride horses in the cowboy movies and to exchange witticisms with tough and experienced men.[7]

After recovering from an automobile accident in 1925, she returned to moviemaking at Mack Sennett's comedy unit where she learned a great deal about slapstick technique. She made the transition to sound movies and by the mid–1930s was known as the queen of the madcap comedies, which included *Hands Across the Table, Twentieth Century*, and *My Man Godfrey*. Made in 1936, *My Man Godfrey* is a good example of screwball comedy.[8] Set in the early days of the depression, the movie featured rich people participating in a treasure hunt as part of a charity event. Lombard played a spoiled socialite who went to the nearest Hooverville (temporary housing set up by unemployed tramps and named after President Hoover) and brought a tramp back to the party as her "find." She won the treasure hunt and convinced her father to give him a job as their butler. "Can you buttle?" she asked him. So Godfrey, played by William Powell, became their man Godfrey. As expected, Lombard fell in love with him, behaved like a silly nitwit throughout, and got what she wanted in the end. When she was not riding her horse into the family library, she was following Godfrey around, nearly driving him crazy with her continuous flow of nonsensical talk. True to 1930s comedies, of course, Godfrey was not really a tramp but a Harvard man down on his luck and thus a suitable marriage mate. The rich family was portrayed as eccentric, while Lombard always looked lovely and lovable while practicing her antics.

DOMESTIC COMICS

Since the home is generally viewed as the natural setting for women, and the multiple mishaps surrounding family life can be treated humorously, domestic comic women are a surefire comedic type. One frequent example is that of the black maid. Beulah, the maid on the radio programs "Fibber McGee and Molly" and "The Beulah Show," is a variant of the filmic image of mammy. Critic Arthur Frank Wertheim called Beulah "a happy-go-lucky maid and mammy type,"[9] while historian J. Fred MacDonald noted that, even after a black woman was finally chosen for the part, it "did not alter the minstrel model upon which the show was based."[10]

Hattie McDaniel, the movie star who had won the Academy Award for her role in *Gone With the Wind* in 1940, became the radio Beulah in the fall of 1947. Beulah laughed easily and would make fun of herself. "I been bendin' over a stove for fifteen years now. (Laughs) The job is new, but the position ain't."[11] She was always congenial and amenable to the demands of her white family. The concerns of the family provided Beulah with her comic opportunities. In the television version, where Ethel Waters and Louise Beavers later played Beulah, she often meddled in family affairs. In a 1952 episode called "Marriage on the Rocks," for example, Beulah read an article about matrimonial problems and concluded that the Hendersons were in trouble. Countless misunderstandings resulted before the situation was cleared up and Beulah was forgiven. In another episode, called "Imagination," Beulah spread the rumor that Mrs. Henderson was expecting a baby, based on erroneous surmises; this caused quite a stir until all was clarified.[12]

Perhaps the greatest practitioner of domestic comedy was Mary Tyler Moore, first as the sweet wife on the "Dick Van Dyke Show" and then as Mary Richards on the "Mary Tyler Moore Show." Born in Brooklyn, New York, in 1937, her family moved to Los Angeles when she was nine years old. She studied dancing, married, had one son, and did minor roles on television. In 1961 she joined the "Dick Van Dyke Show." In this situation comedy, she played Laura Petrie, the wife of Rob Petrie, played by Dick Van Dyke, who was a writer on the Alan Brady Show. The Petries had a son named Richie, and the cast included Carl Reiner as Alan Brady, Rose Marie as a writer for the show, and Morey Amsterdam, her writing partner. Moore's role was secondary to the male principals, and she often was the gentle butt of the humor; she projected a sweet, wholesome image of the earnest wife and mother, the loving Mary, who often got into trouble because of her uncertainty about the role of mother. The domestic comic, as depicted by Moore in this part, was analogous to the nitwit. Child rearing involved comic crises as did wifely chores, and the loving husband was required to solve the problem.[13]

In 1966 the show ended, and Moore went on to movies and the theater, none of which were too successful. In the fall of 1970, she returned to television in the "Mary Tyler Moore Show," a series that became a great success. She played the part of a 30-year-old associate producer in a television newsroom. In the seven years the show ran, Moore's persona gradually changed from the sweet Mary to an independent woman. Supported by a superb cast including Ed Asner as her boss, Lou Grant, Valerie Harper as her neighbor, Rhoda, Cloris Leachman as another neighbor, Phyllis, and Ted Knight as one of her colleagues, the newsroom became a substitute family for the group. Audiences became fond of Mary, her friends, and coworkers. They identified with Rhoda's efforts to lose weight and find a husband, they laughed at Ted's constant bunglings and arrogance, and they enjoyed Mr. Grant's gruff demeanor. Phyllis's pomposity and Betty White's pretentiousness (she played Sue Ann Nivens, the Happy Homemaker for the television station) gave Mary and Lou the opportunity to express witty and wry observations. The domestic comedic style of Moore allowed her to be both subject and object in the humor of each episode. She shared her self-doubts, her fears, and her ignorance with her colleagues and her audience. She displayed a healthy ability to make fun of herself, to be empathic to the foibles of others, and, when necessary, to make fun of silliness. She overcame her diffidence toward Mr. Grant, got the courage to ask him for a raise, and gradually became more self-confident.

Each episode was a masterpiece of comic timing, clever dialogue, and interesting situations. The show remained popular for many years. In 1977 Moore decided to end it while it was still successful and go on to other projects. A testimony to its popularity was the number of people from the show who got their own television show afterward: Harper, Leachman, Knight, and Asner.

As historian Paula S. Fass has noted: "Mary is neither mother nor whore, although she is both supportive and sexually attractive. She is a pal."[14] Mary Tyler Moore's characterization of Mary Richards combined the best aspects of the traditional Mary and Eve images with the newer independent woman. In her analysis of the Moore persona, Fass articulated this notion as well:

No longer locked into traditional categories, the show still never offends. It is a brilliant coup: Instead of painting modern women as men, or substituting pushy women for submissive women and loose women for chaste women, the show transcends traditional categories and emphasizes the core of the American image of virtue.[15]

She concluded by noting that Mary is decent, a decent person and, in so being, wins the love and admiration of her audience. The "Mary Tyler

Moore Show" was that rare example of a successful merger of the dominant images of women; it harked back to traditional values while embracing modern ones.

Domestic comedy is interactive, relying upon the combined talents of all the participants. The genius of Moore was in being a distinctive personality while not being an overpowering one. The humor arose out of daily living with each member of the cast being featured at different times. The ensemble acting was very effective. The other women in the cast sometimes exhibited other comic features: Sue Ann as the nitwit, Rhoda as the self-deprecator, and Phyllis as the sharp tongue.

"All in the Family," a very popular situation comedy of the 1970s that dealt with real-life social issues, also had many spinoffs. One of the most successful, in January of 1975, was "The Jeffersons," the story of a black couple that became financially successful and moved out of a lower-middle-class neighborhood and into an affluent apartment building in Manhattan. Though Sherman Helmsley as George Jefferson was the star of the show, his wife Louise, played by Isabel Sanford, became an important source and provider of the humor. While historian J. Fred MacDonald called her characterization "the resurrection of the loud-but-lovable Mammy," another commentator called her a "wise owl."[16]

Isabel Sanford grew up in New York and appeared in the American Negro Theater. She and her family moved to Los Angeles in 1960. She has been quoted as saying: "There are no black comediennes today. I'm gonna break that mold. I have wanted to be a comedienne, the one who gets all the laughs, all my life. What *The Jeffersons* is for me is a beautiful stepping-stone."[17] The show remained on the air for ten years, testifying to its continued popularity. Sanford as Louise knew how to handle her arrogant and self-satisfied husband. Louise, or Weesie as George called her, would remind him of his roots. When George bragged about how he had fulfilled the American dream, beginning as a little guy with one store and now having seven stores, Louise replied, "Now you're the little guy with seven stores."[18]

When the show began, Sanford looked like the traditional mammy, but as the show continued she lost weight and changed her image. She became attractive, glamorously dressed, and more assertive. Weesie got a job without telling George, and she continually tried to best him in their struggles for power. Misunderstandings and suspicions became the basis for much of the humor. Their neighbors included an interracial couple, and there was a black maid, Florence, played by Marla Gibbs. Contrary to stereotypical expectations, however, Florence was no Beulah. She talked back to her black boss, George, called him shorty, and shot off witty one-liners: "How come we overcame and nobody told me?"[19]

Isabel Sanford and Marla Gibbs became breakthrough comic personalities for black women on television. They were independent women, often working together in collusion against George. They were human with identifiable quirks, foibles, and strengths and fit no preexisting mold for black comics. As Gibbs said of her role: "I feel we break out of stereotypes. I don't take any guff. If Mrs. Jefferson is standing close to the door when the bell rings and tells me to answer it, I say, 'You're closer, you answer it.' "[20] While the humor of "The Jeffersons" operated very much within the domestic comedy framework, the fact that the cast was black, including the woman of the house and the maid, gave it an unusual dimension and an added source of humor.

PHYSICAL COMICS

The woman comedian who uses her body as part of her act may be young and athletic looking or she may be large and powerful. Marie Dressler (1869–1934) was of the latter type. Stout, with dark, menacing eyes, she shoved men around the stage, threw frying pans at them, and received blows in turn. Dressler relied upon her gruff manner and mock seriousness to garner laughs. She once said, "I was born homely and for fifty years it has been my lot to make my living on the stage where the first requisite for a woman's success is supposed to be a face that's easy on the eyes." Since her face and figure did not conform to anyone's standard of beauty, she simply made a face, grimaced at the audience, and made them laugh.[21]

Dressler had a very successful career, first on the musical comedy stage, then in silent film, and still later in sound movies. She was called a "professional jester,"[22] by one observer and had theatrical hits beginning with the 1894 play *The Lady Slavey* in which she played a boisterous music hall singer. A contemporary described her style in this way:

Her humor is just the kind that one would naturally expect to find as a companion to her overflowing physique—ponderous, weighty, and a bit crude, perhaps, but spontaneous, real, and thoroughly good-natured. She never stabs with the keen shaft of cynical wit, and she does no business in the epigram market. Her specialty is incongruity, for Marie Dressler is a burlesquer in thought, word, and deed.[23]

Dressler's persona was usually that of a hapless woman whose yearnings for romance were thwarted. In the Broadway show, *Tillie's Nightmare*, she played a drudge who lived in her mother's boarding house and dreamed of a better life. Her fantasies included a marriage to a rich man, a yachting cruise, and an airplane ride. These scenes were all played comically. Apparently, audiences in 1910 found it funny for large, unattractive women to have such dreams. The play was so successful that it became the basis for five Tillie movies made for Mack Sennett, the well-known comedy director. In the silent film versions, she starred along with Charlie Chaplin and Mabel Normand.[24]

Dressler left moviemaking for about a decade, returning at the end of the 1920s to star in a series of movies with Wallace Beery. *Min and Bill* (1930) and *Tugboat Annie* (1933) became box office hits. The comic trials of this older couple captivated the whole country. They usually played down-and-out people, with Beery always drunk and Dressler trying to reform him. As the *Variety* reviewer said of Min and Bill, "they are rough, tough and slam-bang admirers of each other."[25] Though the audience knew that Min would defend Bill against all outsiders, they also knew that she would beat him up every chance she got in her efforts to change him. The humor was physical, with objects flying around the room with great regularity.

One of Dressler's colleagues in the Mack Sennett comedy unit was another physical comic, Mabel Normand. Dressler described her as "vivaciously pretty and mischievous as a monkey." Normand (1893–1930) was the young, athletic variety of physical comic. She was one of the great pantomimists, clowns, and farceurs of silent film. Normand threw the first cinematic pie into Fatty Arbuckle's face and was considered an equal to Charlie Chaplin in the 11 comedies they made together. At the age of 16, Normand went to the Biograph Studio in New Jersey where the famous director D. W. Griffith was in charge. She began making one-reelers for him with no stage experience whatsoever, one of the very few film stars to do so.[26]

At the Biograph Studio, she met Mack Sennett, the film comedy director, with whom she made most of her successful movies. In 1911 she appeared in Sennett's *The Diving Girl* in which she wore a daring costume consisting of full-length black tights. Against the wishes of her cautious uncle, she did high dives; he then locked her up, only to have her escape and repeat the feat and provide the comedic material for *The Diving Girl*. Normand's comic style was physical, slapstick humor at its best. Working in the medium of moving pictures, she was constantly on the move, falling into water, flying an airplane (she was the first woman to do so in film), and parading in her bathing suit. She was as active as her male companion, running from Keystone Kops, avoiding physical disasters, and looking appealingly helpless when necessary. She behaved like the good sport, the girl next door, as well as the desirable woman. She was always willing to laugh at herself as well as at someone else.[27] In a decade of moviemaking, she made 150 films.

The physical comic who combined this form successfully with screwball and domestic comedy was Lucille Ball, who proved that television is a medium congenial to slapstick women. She became the undisputed queen of television comedy, dominating the field for 25 years. From "I Love Lucy" (1951–57) to "Here's Lucy" (1968–74), she divided her humor between gross hammings and nitwit capers. She regaled generations of television audiences with her sweet deceptions of Desi, her awkward efforts at getting and holding a job, and her elaborate conspiracies with her friend and neighbor Ethel Mertz to outwit their respective husbands. Diana Meehan called Lucy's characterization a "mischievous child-woman."[28] She was the ultimate in irresponsibility, a type not unfamiliar to popular cultural descriptions of comic women.

Born in August 1911 in Butte, Montana, Lucille Ball has recalled that she never laughed as a child and believed that comedians do not laugh.[29] Despite an unhappy childhood and a very bad auto accident as a young woman, she became a dancer in musical theater in the 1920s and then went to Hollywood in the early 1930s. In 1941 she married Cuban bandleader Desi Arnaz. "The only spectacular thing I ever did was eloping to Greenwich and marrying Desi. It happened so fast he had only time to grab a wedding ring in the ten cent store."[30] Their marriage, in exaggerated comic form, became the basis for their very successful television show ten years later. Lucy spent three seasons on CBS radio as the female lead in the situation comedy "My Favorite Husband." On that show, she developed many of the comic mannerisms and themes that she would use on "I Love Lucy." Her scatterbrained persona and easy ability to cry loudly every time something went wrong became part of her style.

The 1951 premier of "I Love Lucy" featured Lucy and Desi (called Ricky on the show) as a happily married couple; Ricky was a bandleader, later an owner of a nightclub and then a television personality, whose wife Lucy was always trying to get into show business. They lived in an apartment building where their next-door neighbors were Fred and Ethel Mertz (played by William Frawley and Vivian Vance). In 1953, when Lucy gave birth to her real son, Desi junior (Ricky junior on television), they had the largest television audience to that date.

The show never dropped below third place in audience ratings during its six-year run. Viewers remembered many favorite episodes; indeed, in the summer of 1958, CBS asked people to send in the name of their favorite Lucy skit as they planned a special to include ten of the most favorite. The audience response was so great that CBS ended up including 13 episodes on the special. One constant theme was Lucy's efforts to get into Ricky's nightclub and later television show. In one episode, she maneuvered her way onto his show to do a cough medicine commercial only to get drunk sampling the product. In another favorite, Lucy decided to bake bread from scratch; she put two whole packages of yeast into the dough and ended up getting pinned to the far wall of the kitchen when the bread was released from the oven.

In 1960 Lucy and Desi divorced, thus ending one of television's most successful marriages. She returned in 1962 with "The Lucy Show" where her children Luci and Desi played roles as did Vivian Vance and Gale Gordon Lucy's sour-faced boss. In her next series, "Here's Lucy," she and Gale Gordon were featured. Although these latter two series were popular, they did not match the incredible success of "I Love Lucy." The persona of Lucille Ball was muted in these two situation comedies; she relied more on verbal comedy and gave up the physical humor, the sight gags, and the distorted facial expressions that she had perfected on "I Love Lucy."[31]

Lucy was the funny, somewhat scatterbrained, female whose foxy and childlike qualities endeared her to all ages and both sexes. It was her uncanny ability to capture both the allegedly childish qualities of the woman with the shrewdness assigned to men. Lucy won sympathy from the audience since she portrayed women as dependent, yet aware of their status. Her comedic genius drew from many of the women comics of earlier years as well. Her nitwit style had ties to Mabel Normand and Constance Talmadge, her grotesque grimaces linked her to Marie Dressler, and her fast-talking, wisecracking pose resembled her friend Carole Lombard's style. Lucy also borrowed from the best of the silent film comedians such as Charlie Chaplin and Buster Keaton. The intimacy of the television screen seemed perfectly harmonious with her style. Her expressive face and flexible dancer's body were captured on television. Ball understood the new medium, placed the cameras strategically (in fact, she was the first to use three cameras in one scene so as to edit the film effectively afterward), and amalgamated all of the tried-and-true comic techniques to make herself the most recognized face on television.

Carol Burnett, born in San Antonio, Texas, in 1934, is often considered the successor to Lucille Ball. Her series, the "Carol Burnett Show," began in 1966 and remained a very popular comedy and variety show until Burnett decided to end the series in 1978. In contrast to Ball's situation comedies, Burnett's show resembled vaudeville's variety shows. She had weekly guests as well as a regular cast (Harvey Korman, Vicki Lawrence, and Tim Conway) with whom she performed in skits and musical numbers. But like Lucille Ball, Burnett combined physical comedy with screwball and domestic comedy.[32]

Burnett grew up in Los Angeles and was an avid moviegoer who fantasized about being in show business. In the fall of 1959, she went on the "Garry Moore Show" where she did comic routines. Her comic style included grotesque exaggerations or distortions of stock characters. For example, she did an interpretation of Cinderella as a raucous woman with a hangover. She usually deemphasized her pleasant looks, hamming it up, making ugly faces, wearing wigs, slouching, and generally appearing as an awkward duckling. As one critic noted: "If she wears a wig, it is invariably snatched off, revealing her own flattened hair beneath. Every crafty thought, base motive, ache of hangover and trembling hope is so pitiably naked that it commands excruciating sympathy."[33] Another commentator labeled Burnett a member of the "gargoyle school of comedy" where her compatriots were Martha Raye, Imogene Coca, and Nancy Walker."[34]

On her show, Burnett developed a number of personas that became audience favorites and were regularly on view: Burnett as the old, forgetful wife of Harvey Korman, as his carping wife, with Vicki Lawrence playing her bossy mother, and as a cleaning woman, wearing baggy clothes and appearing as the hapless person, a typical comedic pose. Loyal fans tuned in Saturday nights just as they had watched Lucy faithfully on Monday nights. Within the weekly skits, the domestic comedy mode prevailed, while in other parts of the show, Burnett sang, played in other skits with her guests, or, at the opening of each show, talked directly to her audience. There has been no successor to her brand of humor on contemporary television.

SELF-DEPRECATORS

While all of the above comics had, as one element in their comic routines, a self-deprecating quality, the self-deprecators rely most heavily and constantly on this characteristic. Their weaknesses occupy center stage in their performances. They are the subjects and objects of their humor. Self-deprecators can appear as solo artists on nightclub stages, or they can function within a domestic comedy setting. A good example of the latter type was Valerie Harper's role as Rhoda, first on the "Mary Tyler Moore Show," and then on her own television series, "Rhoda." Harper's humor arose from her self-doubts, her obsessive interest in her appearance, and her dogged determination to get married. She emphasized her low self-esteem, allowing audiences to laugh at her announced weaknesses and vulnerabilities.

Harper, born in Suffern, New York, in 1940, began acting in improvisational comic clubs after high school. In 1970 she joined the new "Mary Tyler Moore Show" and, four years later, began her own series. The opening statement describing herself said it all:

My name is Rhoda Morgenstern. I was born in the Bronx, New York in December of 1941. I've always felt responsible for World War II. The first thing that I remember liking that liked me back was food. I had a bad puberty, it lasted seventeen years. I'm a high school graduate. I went to art school—my entrance exam was on a book of matches. I decided to move out of the house when I was 24. My mother still refers to this as the time I ran away from home. Eventually, I ran to Minneapolis where it's cold and I figured I'd keep better. Now I'm back in Manhattan. New York, this is your last chance.[35]

During the four-year history of "Rhoda," she married Joe Gerard, played by David Groh, and separated from him after the start of the 1976 season. The writers of the show found it difficult to sustain a comedy based upon Rhoda being happily married; after all, her self-deprecating style rested on the unhappiness of the comic. Satisfaction destroyed Rhoda's ability to be self-doubting. Indeed, while Rhoda was still happily married, her sister

Brenda, played by Julie Kavner, was brought in to be a younger, earlier version of Rhoda: she was overweight and obsessed with marriage. In the final season of the show, Rhoda went to work for the Doyle Costume Company, had a new boy friend, and tried to no avail to recapture the show's earlier vitality and the audience ratings.

As a solo self-deprecator, Joan Rivers stands out. Since her first appearance in 1965 on Johnny Carson's "Tonight Show," she gained popularity in nightclubs and frequent appearances as host of his show as a self-mocker. The willingness of Rivers to discuss her small breasts, her inadequate love life with her husband Edgar, and her insecurities made her distinctive. She has said of her comic persona: "I love that woman up there because she's so common and so vulgar. . . . I do all that for shock values, and it really works. . . . However, I wouldn't want to be that woman's friend. I wouldn't want her at my dinner party."[36]

Joan Rivers became famous when, at the beginning of her monologue, she asked her audience, "Can We Talk?" She used the audience as material for her routines, incorporating their replies into her stories. Rivers mocked herself, the woman's yearnings to be ever young, and the foibles of the famous. She became a critic of others as well as herself. She insulted the actress Elizabeth Taylor in the late 1970s when Taylor became overweight. The more outrageous her remarks were, the better Rivers liked it. Her acerbic wit tested the limits of television's endurance. In this respect, Rivers resembles the bawdy women entertainers and is also a bridge to the satirists. She has noted:

You have to be abrasive to be a current comic. If you don't offend somebody, you become pap. I think ten percent of the people should just hate me. . . . Humor is tasteless. These are tasteless times. . . . Truth is vicious, but why can't we say it. The question is—who is going to tell the emperor he's not wearing clothes? I think that's my job. I'm expressing what people think—and they love it.[37]

Rivers has kept an extensive and elaborate card file of her material. She categorizes all of her jokes according to subject and finds that nothing is beyond the boundaries of her self-imposed tastelessness. As a self-deprecator who also attacks everyone else, Joan Rivers moves into the final category of women comics as well, the satirists. The best example of independent women in comedy can be found in the satirists, a type rare among male and female comics. Satire requires an astute intelligence, knowledge of social conditions, and a bold ability to translate critical opinions into humorous words. All of the women comics described possessed the intelligence essential to satire, but their talents and propensities favored other expressions.

SATIRISTS

Like self-deprecators, satirists can be found in situation comedy or as solo performers. Perhaps the best earlier practitioner of satire was Fanny Brice (1891–1951). Using her featured skit in the Ziegfeld Follies as the setting, she created characters, situations, and themes that commented on the role of women as well as cultural life in New York. The satirist, after all, is a social critic, a commentator on life around her. As show business historian Robert Toll has written of her art, "Even in her satires and parodies, she was an eminently humane comedienne, sensitive to the feelings of the people and the characters she laughed at."[38] Brice wrote about comedy:

If you're a comic you have to be nice. And the audience has to like you. You have to have a softness about you, because if you do comedy and you are harsh, there is something offensive about it. Also you must set up your audience for the laugh you are working for. So you go along and everything is fine, like any other act, and then—boom! you give it to them. Like there is a beautiful painting of a woman and you paint a mustache on her.[39]

Her ability to spoof popular people, ideas, and shows of her day endeared her to the audiences. From 1910 to 1923, with one year off, she appeared in the Ziegfeld Follies in New York. She had a lovely singing voice that she used in a conventional way in the first verse, but by the second chorus she changed her tone, mood, and style. Brice then turned the song into a satire. She made fun of others as well as the persona she had been in the first verse. When she sang "I'm an Indian," for example, she dressed in costume, appeared as an authentic, lovely young Indian woman only to destroy the illusion by assuming a Yiddish accent in the second chorus and calling herself Rosie Rosenstein, a nice Jewish girl who somehow landed on an Indian reservation.[40] By stepping out of character, she shared with her audience the fact that she was performing and that she was more than the part she played.

Though born into a New York Jewish family, Brice did not know Yiddish. It was only through the suggestion of composer Irving Berlin that she learned the Yiddish intonations and added them to her repertory. She was one of four children who discovered her singing voice as a child; combined with her histrionic personality, she could not be held back. Brice sang at amateur nights in Brooklyn as a child where the voluntary contributions of the audience made her a rich little girl. In 1909, while performing in the musical comedy, *College Girls*, she was seen by a Ziegfeld representative and was hired for the Follies. At the age of 18, she was on her way.[41]

The songs of Brice became seriocomic routines in which she created a whole environment in each one. "Second Hand Rose," which became one of her great hits, described a young woman who always had to settle for used objects. Her father was in the secondhand business; so her clothes and the family furniture were all things that had been used before. The height of indignity, she revealed, was that the man she loved had been married before. Brice often portrayed herself as the hapless victim, a typical comic pose; she became the long-suffering woman who had to tolerate much disappointment in her life. "Oy, How I Hate That Fellow Nathan" was a self-deprecating song in which she described a lover who treated her badly; though he promised to marry her, he could not think far enough ahead to set the date. Nathan said he would lay down and die for her, but, she noted, he would not stand up and work for her.

Brice sang songs that simultaneously declared woman's love for a man while satirizing the male ego. She could spoof her own devotion in "Cooking Breakfast for the One I Love" or sing it straight in "I'd Rather Be Blue Over You than Happy with Someone Else." She counseled her audiences to be brave and take the good with the bad in "If You Want the Rainbow You Must Have Rain." In other routines she made famous at the Ziegfeld Follies, Brice satirized the modern dance movement, evangelical preachers, and serious drama. She made fun of the Romeo and Juliet story and mocked doting mothers in "Becky is Back in the Ballet."

In interviews and in a biography published after her death, Fanny Brice said that she could be satirical because she never took herself seriously and never saw herself as above the audience. She identified with them and they knew it. Her fans enjoyed her exposure of human weaknesses because they knew she presented them with love, not bitterness. The critics shared the audience's love of a Brice performance. According to Brooks Atkinson of the *New York Times*: "Fanny is in top form. Early in the show you will discover her introducing the huckster's note into evangelical racketeering with a song entitled 'Soul Saving Sadie.' Toward the end of the first act she is Countess Dubinsky, who right down to her skinsky is working for Minsky, whereupon she performs a hilarious travesty upon the sinful fan dance."[42]

A critic in the *New York World-Telegram* wrote: "her quivering voice, her slyly savage imitation of a creaky voiced singer of red hot songs, her bewildered Jewish Juliet, rocked this reviewer with laughs—and he has heard it time and again."[43] By the mid-1920s, however, Brice had tired of the regular performances and tried Broadway and the movies, but neither suited her talents. In the 1930s, she began doing a child-rascal character named Baby Snooks on radio shows and later had her own radio show centered around that personality.

When she performed in the Follies, Fanny Brice was an inimitable performer of satire. A television example of the type was Bea Arthur who played Maud, a loud-mouthed critic of everything. From 1972 to 1978, the "Maud" show was a popular avenue for social satire. Controversial topics such as abortion, women's rights, racism, and sexuality were discussed with Maud contributing her biting and outspoken comments. Her husband on the show was Walter, played by Bill Macy, and he was often the butt of her humor. Framed within a domestic comedy, the biting satire borrowed its style from "All in the Family," the pacesetter of this genre.

Maud attacked rather than reacted to the humor of others. She appeared as a self-confident, mature woman who had opinions on all subjects. Her quick wit and brashness became the female equivalent of Archie Bunker, the star of "All in the Family." In the 1970s, it became fashionable to spoof serious subjects of the 1960s. While blacks and women marched for their rights in the prior decade, Maud assumed women's equality and joked about everyone and everything else.

Of the five categories of women comics described, the domestic comics, physical comics, and satirists most often exhibited independent woman traits. The nitwits emphasized their silliness and their dependence upon males for help; the self-deprecators exhibited their weaknesses, not their strengths. While domestic comics like Mary Tyler Moore as Laurie Petrie were submissive, in her own show as Mary Richards, Moore became increasingly independent and willing to go on the attack in her humor. Similarly, Isabel Sanford as Louise took on George Jefferson more and more as the years went by. The physical comics who combined domestic and screwball features such as Lucille Ball and Carol Burnett demonstrated their unique and independent qualities in their very willingness to expose themselves to ridicule. Physical comic Marie Dressler, on the other hand, always integrated her spunky independence into her physical comedy. Her beating up of Wallace Beery, though designed to arouse laughter, was also an assertion of independence. The satirists, of course, appeared as confident commentators on social mores. Collectively, they presented their audiences with laughing and liberating views of women's images.

NOTES

1. Constance Talmadge, "The Tragedy of Being Funny," *Motion Picture*, August 1927, p. 102. See also De Witt Bodeen, "Constance Talmadge," *Films in Review*, December 1967, pp. 613–30.

2. Allene Talmey, *Doug and Mary and Others* (New York: Macy-Masius, 1927), p. 46.

3. Joe Franklin, *Encyclopedia of Comedians* (Secaucus, N.J.: Citadel Press, 1979), p. 82.

4. Arthur Frank Wertheim, *Radio Comedy* (New York: Oxford University Press, 1979), pp. 200–1.

5. Ibid., p. 203.

6. Ibid.

7. The entry in *Notable American Women* by Alan S. Downer (Cambridge, Mass.: Belknap Press, Volume 2, 1971, pp. 425–26) provides the biographical information on Lombard.

8. The *New York Times Film Review* is an invaluable source for analysis of films, though nothing replaces viewing the movie.

9. Wertheim, *Radio Comedy*, p. 238.

10. J. Fred MacDonald, *Don't Touch That Dial!: Radio Programming in American Life from 1920 to 1960* (Chicago: Nelson-Hall, 1979), p. 101.

11. Wertheim, *Radio Comedy*, p. 238.

12. I viewed both episodes of the 1952 "Beulah Show," ABC-TV.

13. Vincent Terrace's *The Complete Encyclopedia of Television Programs 1947–1979* (New York: A. S. Barnes, 1980) is useful. Arthur Hough, "Trials and Tribulations— Thirty Years of Sitcom," in *Understanding Television*, ed. Richard P. Adler (New York: Praeger, 1981), pp. 201–23, is a good overview of situation comedies.

14. Paula S. Fass, "Television as Cultural Document: Promises and Problems," in *Television as a Cultural Force*, eds. Richard Adler and Douglass Cater (New York: Praeger, 1976), p. 41.

15. Ibid., pp. 41–42.

16. J. Fred MacDonald, *Blacks and White TV: Afro-Americans in Television since 1948* (Chicago: Nelson-Hall, 1983), p. 177, and Rick Mitz, *The Great TV Sitcom Book* (New York: Richard Marek, 1980), p. 344.

17. Mitz, *Great TV Sitcom Book*, p. 346.

18. Joel Eisner and David Krinsky, *Television Comedy Series: An Episode Guide to 153 TV Sitcoms in Syndication* (Jefferson, N.C.: McFarland, 1984), pp. 417–24, and Mitz, *Great TV Sitcom Book*, p. 344.

19. Mitz, p. 344.

20. Ibid., p. 346.

21. Quoted in William Cahn, *A Pictorial History of the Great Comedians* (New York: Grosset and Dunlap, 1970), p. 122.

22. Lewis C. Strang, *Prima Donnas and Soubrettes of Light Opera and Musical Comedy in America* (Boston: L.C. Page, 1900), p. 183.

23. Ibid., p. 182.

24. Other sources that discuss the career of Dressler are David Ewen, *New Complete Book of the American Musical Theater* (New York: Oxford University Press, 1970), Gerald Bordman, *American Musical Theater: A Chronicle* (New York: Oxford University Press, 1978), and the entry in *Notable American Women* by Albert E. Johnson (1971), vol. 1, pp. 519–21.

25. Bige, "Min and Bill," *Variety*, November 26, 1930).

26. Wallace Evan Davies' essay on Normand in *Notable American Women* vol. 1 is a basic source as is the two-part essay on Mack Sennett by Robert Giroux in *Films in Review* (December 1968 and January 1969).

27. The reviews of Normand's films in the *New York Times Film Review* summarize the plots and the comic style of her movies. See also Kalton C. Lahue and Terry Brewer, *Keystone Kops and Custards: The Legend of Keystone Films* (Norman: University of Oklahoma Press, 1968).

28. Diana M. Meehan, *Ladies of the Evening: Women Characters of Prime Time Television* (Metuchen, N.J.: Scarecrow Press, 1983), p. 21.

29. There are many sources on Lucille Ball. One of the early ones is Herb Howe, "The Lady That's Known as Luci," *Photoplay*, March 1947, pp. 56–59, 84–86. Another is Eleanor Harris, *The Real Story of Lucille Ball* (New York: Farrar Straus & Young with Ballantine Books, 1954).

30. Howe, "Luci," p. 86.

31. Tim Brooks and Earle Marsh, *The Complete Directory of Prime Time Network TV Shows, 1946-Present* (New York: Ballentine Books, 1979) is a valuable source as are Gilbert Seldes, "Comical Gentlewomen," *Saturday Review*, May 2, 1953, and "Don't Laugh When You Call Me President," *McCalls, March 1963.*

32. Brooks and Marsh, Complete Directory, pp. 106–7, describes the show.

33. Cahn, *Pictorial History,* p. 187.

34. Edith Efron, "The Girl in the Rubber Mask," in *TV Guide: The First Twenty Five Years,* ed. Jay S. Harris, in association with the editors of *TV Guide* (New York: Simon and Schuster, 1978), p. 73.

35. Quoted in Terrace, *Complete Encyclopedia,* p. 831.

36. Richard Meryman, "Can We Talk? Why Joan Rivers Can't Stop," *McCalls,* September 1983, p. 63.

37. Ibid., p. 64. Another good source is Lee Israel, "Joan Rivers and How She Got That Way," *Ms.,* October 1984, pp. 109–14.

38. Robert C. Toll, *On With the Show: The First Century of Show Business* (New York: Oxford University Press, 1976), p. 323.

39. Quoted in Cahn, *Pictorial History,* p. 67.

40. Brice's record albums capture her comedic style. Among the ones I listened to are *Fanny Brice* (Audio Fidelity Records, 1968) and *Fanny Brice/Helen Morgan (RCA Victor LPV–561, 1969).*

41. Norman Katkov, The Fabulous Fanny: The Story of Fanny Brice (New York: Alfred Knopf, 1953), offers a good summary of her life and career.

42. Quoted in ibid., p. 237.

43. Quoted in ibid., pp. 243–44.

7

Adventurers: An Atypical Form

Women adventurers, by definition, are unusual and rare independent women. They are seekers of excitement, daring women willing to face unexpected challenges. They are novel blendings of male and female characteristics. Women adventurers visit foreign, intriguing places where they experience danger and often face death. True, they often have the aid of stalwart men to save them, but they defy cultural stereotyping. They exhibit courage, physical skill, willingness to sacrifice, stamina, and grace under pressure. As a result, they are found only in limited quantity throughout popular culture.

Women adventurers come in two basic types: as young women and, even rarer, as adult women. The teenager, for example, does not disrupt the culture's role expectations for women; therefore, before settling down to domesticity, it is acceptable for Nancy Drew to have adventures. The implicit assumption is that, when she grows up, she will marry Ned Nickerson and raise a family. Because danger is closely associated with adventure, women cannot be permitted such activity. Though the days of chivalry are long gone, the assumption still prevails that women are not capable of handling weapons. Further, it is believed that they are physically unable to overpower men. It is only in recent years that these realities and accompanying myths have come into question, and subsequently the images may change in the near future.

Pearl White (1890–1938) became the prototypical young woman adventurer in silent film serials. Born in Greenridge, Missouri, she dropped out of high school during her sophomore year, joined a local stock company, and at the age of 18, left home to travel with a theatrical company. From there, she went into silent filmmaking, particularly the new serials. These multiepisodic stories appeared on the screen before the feature and were well suited to suspense and adventure. Most were designed as cliffhangers; that is, the heroine, hanging over the cliff and screaming for her life, is left in that position until next week.[1]

In 1914 Pearl White starred in *The Perils of Pauline*, 20 episodes in which she escaped from sinking boats, houses on fire, auto accidents, and villainous men. In contrast to most serials, each adventure usually was resolved at the end of each episode, or chapter as it was called. In this serial, White played a rich young woman who wished to write rather than marry. However, besides her hero's persistent attentions, she had to avoid the constant dangers she faced from her late father's secretary who was trying to kill her and inherit the family fortune. In the opening installment, the crisis was left unresolved to lure audiences back into the theater. As one contemporary critic noted, "it is clearly to her interest to elope with almost anyone; but what she really does do is left undecided as yet until the next of the series."[2]

The Perils of Pauline became so popular that a song was written that same year describing her exploits. The writer pitied poor Pauline who drifted out to sea, was tied to a tree, thrown over a cliff, dynamited in a submarine, and locked in a den with a hungry lion. "Poor Pauline!" concluded the song.[3] Her audience, consisting mainly of youngsters, thrilled to her every adventure. White wore a blonde wig and did her own stunts, many of which were filmed in New York City with crowds surrounding the film crew. In 1914–15 she followed up her success with *The Exploits of Elaine*, consisting of 14 episodes. In this serial, she played Elaine Dodge, an "ingenue and athlete—the thoroughly modern type of girl," as the printed introduction to the serial said. Elaine searched for her father's murderer, a man known as "Clutching Hand." She had the assistance of detective Craig Kennedy who explained scientific matters to her and appeared at convenient times to save her. In one episode, titled "The Life Current," Elaine was pronounced dead only to be brought back to life by Kennedy's vast knowledge of science.[4]

The Elaine serial was so well received that it was followed by *The New Exploits of Elaine* (1915) and *The Romance of Elaine* (1915). As the United States prepared for war, White made a propaganda serial called *Pearl of the Army* (1916–17) in which she fought the "Silent Menace" who was trying to steal the secret plans for the defense of the Panama Canal. In a rousing conclusion, White kept the flag flying and knocked the Menace off of the roof. Other serials were *The Fatal Ring* (1919), *The House of Hate* (1918), *The Lightning Raider* (1919), and finally *The Black Secret* (1919–20).

In 1922 Pearl White decided to continue making serials only to discover that an old back injury made it impossible for her to do her own stunts. A double was used and unfortunately was killed during the performance of a stunt. This event effectively ended the serial-making career of Pearl White. But during the years 1914–20 no one was more popular; it was estimated that she had an audience of 15 million people including fans in Europe and Japan.[5] Pearl White conveyed the image of a constantly active, adventuresome young woman willing to face the unknown in any setting. Just as the new one-reeler silent film moved, so she moved incessantly, and in so doing projected the impression that young women were physically active and capable of all feats.

Though Pearl White had few successors in sound movies or radio, there were other interesting, though minor, examples of the type. During the 1940s, there was a serial heroine who "swung through the trees on vines, battled fearlessly with diamond hunters and gorillas, and, when captured and powerless, graciously let her boy friend save her."[6] Audiences watched 15 episodes of *Jungle Girl* in 1941, 15 episodes of the *Perils of Nyoka* (1942), and 13 episodes of *Jungle Queen* (1945). Republic Pictures tried to recapture the market that had adored the *Perils of Pauline* serial, but as one analyst noted:

After all, the serials were now primarily made for young boys, and young boys knew that women were too fragile to engage in the strenuous activity demanded of a serial star. A heroine was necessary only as someone to be placed in peril, and as someone to be repeatedly hit over the head so that she would not be in the path of the hero's swinging fists.[7]

Women adventurers in the 1940s serials became subordinate to the hero; contrary to the confident role played by Pauline, Nyoka screamed a lot, was trapped in difficult situations, and was rescued by the hero, Tom Neal.[8] It is an interesting commentary that while the real-life women's suffrage movement of the 1910s seemed to give credibility to Pauline's escapades, the real-life working of 1940s women in new and unusual occupations (Rosie the Riveter during the war) did not encourage the jungle queens to initiate adventures or take charge of their situations.

In the very popular cowboy serials of the 1940s, women played ancillary roles. Gail Davis supported Gene Autry as did Dale Evans to Roy Rogers. When westerns appeared on television in the 1950s and 1960s, they retained the same formula. Adult women performed regularly only on 3 of the 15 most popular westerns between 1955 and 1965: "Lawman," "Gunsmoke," and "Wyatt Earp."[9] Kitty on "Gunsmoke," the most promising female character in a television western, had her role decreased after initial episodes suggested an Eve-like image. Mothers protested that family television should not depict frontier prostitutes; Kitty became the asexual friend of Matt Dillon and the entrepreneur of a saloon where the barmaids presumably only served liquor. She was an independent, self-supporting woman, surely a worthy image, but she gave up her Eve qualities to placate conservative voices. She also displayed no adventuring, risk-taking characteristics. These were restricted to the cowboys.

Adult women adventurers appeared in the movies of the 1950s, most notably in films with Joan Crawford and Barbara Stanwyck. As mature women, they became ranch owners who went up against the bad men. In *Cattle Queen of Montana* (1954), *The Maverick Queen* (1956), and *Forty Guns* (1957), Stanwyck carried a whip, fought Indians, and saved the ranch. In *Johnny Guitar* (1954), Joan Crawford was a saloon owner who survived in the Wild West. The West, which was the adventuring territory of man, rarely held women except as the civilizers, the Marys, the schoolmarms, or the Eves. Thus, the unusual Stanwyck and Crawford roles in male preserves only demonstrated the rarity of the event. Apparently, the older woman was above the traditional stereotypes and could enter the man's arena without challenging his dominance.

Stanwyck continued her screen role as a western leader in the television series of the 1950s, "The Big Valley." As the matriarch Victoria Barkley, she presided over a large ranch in the San Joaquin Valley with her four grown sons. However, rather than be the active force, she usually became the victim who required rescuing. She used persuasion to gain her objectives and left the adventuring to her sons.[10]

One female movie star of the early 1970s emerged as the exceptional woman adventurer: Pam Grier. Beautiful, black Grier made a brief, but successful, career out of playing "tough mammas," black women who beat men up and destroyed the enemy. Grier had hoped for a richer, and more diverse, film career. Born to a noncommissioned officer in the U.S. Air Force, she grew up on a variety of bases in Europe. The family eventually settled in Denver, and while still a teenager, she entered a beauty contest and was spotted by a Hollywood agent. Her film career began with small roles in mediocre movies, followed by the series of "tough mamma" roles. By the mid-1970s, that image, however unusual it first appeared to be, lost its audience appeal and Grier's career ground to a halt.[11]

A black woman starring in any movie was clearly unusual; especially unique was a physically powerful black woman. As critic Mark Jacobson described her movies:

Pam has made a living out of beating up men. She gun-butted them in *Black Mamma, White Mamma*, cast voodoo spells over them in *Scream, Blacula, Scream*, and speared them in *The Arena*. In *Coffy*, Pam was at her most outgoing: she blasted a pusher's head off, stabbed a kinky hit man with a bobby pin, ran a Mafioso over in a Dodge, and blew away three different sets of genitals with a double-barreled shot-gun.[12]

Grier's films were profitable though criticized by both blacks and whites as "blaxploitation," films that portrayed black people in a negative light. The unrealism of the black mammy portrait was replaced with the militant, forceful one of a tough mamma, an equally unrealistic image. Other images seemed unavailable to black women in the popular media. Tamara Dobson, another powerfully built, tall, black actress played the same type of woman in *Cleopatra Jones*; in it, she destroyed a drug ring run by both whites and blacks.

Television continued the popular formula adventure shows; in addition to the western, the detective and spy show became very common. From 1955 to 1965, there were 17 detective shows, but only 6 had regular female roles.[13] Women were usually the victims or the sexual diversions within this formula. Rarely were they the active brains of the operation or the physically powerful adventurers. Women were to be protected from danger. However, occasionally, in television's search for success, a popular show spawned a host of imitators. In 1967 NBC launched "The Girl from U.N.C.L.E.," hoping to benefit from its earlier success, "The Man from U.N.C.L.E.." Stefanie Powers played April Dancer who, in concert with her male partner, Mark Slate, played by Noel Harrison, worked for U.N.C.L.E., an international organization committed to destroying its enemy, T.H.R.U.S.H., an evil conspiracy.

The show was done as a spoof of the international spy thriller, with Powers often acting as if she did not quite believe in the plausibility of the stories. In one episode called "The Catacomb and Dogma Affair," she and her partner stopped thieves from stealing jewels owned by the Vatican.[14] Powers demonstrated both her considerable beauty in Eve-like actions to lure the bad guys as well as martial skills to elude her captors. Her obvious intelligence also was projected, though the silliness of the stories and the unlikely teaming of Powers with an English actor doomed the series to failure. It lasted only one season.

A more successful show, "Mod Squad," began in September 1968 and lasted five seasons. This show modified the detective formula by featuring three young probationers, each from a different class and background: one black young man, a rich, white male dropout, and the daughter of a prostitute. The female, played by Peggy Lipton, was part of the team but was not the central character in the adventure. Indeed, the main purpose of the show, as noted by some observers, was to coopt the youth movement of the late 1960s.[15] The "Mod Squad" often infiltrated countercultural institutions in order to catch the evil adults who corrupted young people, a contemporary adaptation of an old formula.

Women adventurers appeared on 1970s television in unprecedented numbers. Television programmers, always conscious of the changing marketplace, took note of the fact that more women were going to college, joining the work force, and espousing sympathy for women's rights. They acknowledged this new reality by bringing women into adventure as undercover agents, detectives, and women with special powers. The stars of "The Bionic Woman," "Wonder Woman," and "Police Woman" all hid their true identities. They often appeared as Eves, luring their prey into the police net, a new twist on an old theme. The new feminism of the 1970s may have created a raised consciousness among the population as to the capabilities of women, yet that very same audience still held conventional views about women, their proper roles, and the expected images. Thus, in this clever, and typical, ploy of popular culture writers, audiences had it both ways: fantasy wishes for excitement and danger were satisfied, while few women departed from expected roles and behavior.

Angie Dickinson as Sargent Pepper Martin in "Police Woman" used her attractive figure to pose as a call girl or a gangster's moll to ensnare the criminals.[16] The show went on television in September 1974 and was a popular series for four years. Assisted by Earl Holliman who played Lieutenant Bill Crowley, as well as two male detectives, Dickinson acted as part of an undercover team of the Los Angeles Poice Department. The team worked on vice cases primarily, giving ample opportunity for Dickinson to display her appealing body. Despite this consideration, she still qualified as an adventuring woman. She used a gun effectively, faced danger frequently, and acted as an equal to her male colleagues. Angie Dickinson's pleasing personality, strong but not militant, attracted an audience at a time when the women's liberation movement was in full sway.

"The Bionic Woman," starring Lindsay Wagner, premiered in January 1976 and remained on the air for two years. The show was a spinoff from "The Six Million Dollar Man" where the bionic woman, known as Jamie Somers, first appeared. After suffering a very bad sky diving accident, Somers was reconstructed bionically. She developed miraculous powers in her legs, one arm possessed superior strength, and an ear had acute long-distance hearing. While acting as a teacher, she performed special assignments for the Office of Scientific Information. She fought spies, smugglers, kidnappers, and several times, extraterrestial creatures. Occasionally, Steve Austin, the six million dollar bionic man, appeared on the show. But mainly, Wagner, as the bionic woman, performed the feats of strength and adventure—thanks to medical science.

A mythic woman adventurer, taken from comic strips, was "Wonder Woman." Played by Lynda Carter, the series began in March 1976 and stayed on the air until the spring of 1981. Carter, who stands 5 feet 11 inches, offered a convincing portrait of the Amazon who fought Nazis and helpted Major Steven Trevor fend off numerous dangers. In the second season, the setting became contemporary, and Wonder Woman now faced terrorists and subversives. She worked with Steve Trevor, Jr., a dead ringer for his father; Wonder Woman, of course, never aged.

Lynda Carter interpreted her role as Wonder Woman as one in which she became a positive role model to young women. "I try to impress upon young girls," she said, "that they can be anything they want to be. It isn't how you look that's important. It's how you use whatever you have that's important—your interests and talents."[17] Collectively, all three television series provided vicarious pleasure in seeing women in the world face danger and experience excitement. Commentators talked about role models for women, the remarks of Lynda Carter demonstrate her awareness of that notion. Young girls growing up did not have to become detectives or bold adventurers, but they could learn from the show the value of personal strength, decisiveness, and courage. Despite the popularity of these three series, their success was built upon assumptions that never challenged cultural views about women. Their independence was limited. Jamie Somers had bionic parts, and Wonder Woman was a mythic Amazon. They were not real women; therefore, they could perform manly feats. Police Woman always had able male assistance when the going got rough.

Another series that premiered in September 1974, the same year as "Police Woman," did not have as happy a fate. "Get Christie Love!" starred an attractive black actress named Teresa Graves as an undercover detective with the Los Angeles Police Department. She was a streetwise woman, capable of defending herself against the criminals. The characterization was closer to the tough black mamma image of Pam Grier than to the more conventional Eve-independent persona of Angie Dickinson. Audiences did not watch the show, which went off the air after only one season.

"Cagney and Lacey," a show featuring two women detectives for the New York Police Department, debuted in 1982 and after a shaky start became a popular television series. Cagney, played by Sharon Gless, was blonde, attractive, single, and a feminist while Lacey, played by Tyne Daley, was married, a mother of three (she became pregnant and had the child during the 1986 season), and more traditional. The contrasts, as well as the frequent compromises they agreed upon, provided an exciting and dramatic setting for the weekly episodes. "Cagney and Lacey" dealt with difficult social issues as well: breast cancer, abortion, homosexuality, and alcoholism. The personality and philosophical differences between the protagonists reflected the multiple perspectives of women in the 1980s. This show captured the diversity within the adventure format.

Notwithstanding the portrayal of women adventurers on television, the type remains a minor image in comparison to the more pervasive romantic heroine, the comic in all of its variety, and the career woman. The view of woman risking her life in dangerous situations, encountering physical violence, and grappling with evil men is unacceptable to most people and therefore receives little attention in popular fantasies. Popular culture confirms acceptable dreams, affirms our basic values, and encourages our happiest thoughts. Women adventurers only become acceptable to the popular taste when there are strong men present to reassert the proper power relationships and protect the women. The continued success of "Cagney and Lacey," a sole representative of women adventurers without supporting men in the late 1980s, only attests to its atypicality. Women adventurers are novelties, not essential or expected images in popular culture. Despite the success of many aspects of the women's movement in the 1960s and 1970s, the fundamental conservatism of the culture asserts itself in its popular cultural offerings. Real-life women may study karate and tai kowon do, but fantasy women do not.

NOTES

1. Biographical material on Pearl White can be obtained from the *Notable American Women* entry by Harvey Deneroff, vol. 1 (Cambridge, Mass.: Belknap Press, 1971) pp. 589–90, as well as Wallace E. Davies, "Truth about Pearl White," *Films in Review*, November 1959, pp. 537–48. See also Kalton C. Lahue, *Continued Next Week: A History of the Moving Picture Serial* (Norman: University of Oklahoma Press, 1964).

2. Hanford C. Judson, "1914 Review," reprinted in Anthony Slide, ed., *Selected Film Criticism 1912–1920* (Metuchen, N.J.: Scarecrow Press, 1982), pp. 197–98.

3. Davies, "Pearl White," p. 537.

4. Raymond William Stedman, *The Serials* (Norman: University of Oklahoma Press, 1971), pp. 15–16. Also Lahue, *Contiued Next Week*, pp. 27–28.

5. Davies, "Pearl White," pp. 542–43, and Lahue, *Continued Next Week*, pp. 41–42.

6. Raymond William Stedman, *The Serials: Suspense and Drama by Installment*, 2nd ed. (Norman: University of Oklahoma Press, 1977), p. 132.

7. Alan G. Barbour, *Days of Thrills and Adventure* (New York: Collier Books, 1970), p. 101.

8. Ibid.

9. Diana M. Meehan, *Ladies of the Evening: Women Characters of Prime-Time Television* (Metuchen, N.J.: Scarecrow Press, 1983), p. 109.

10. Ibid., pp. 102–3.

11. Molly Haskell has written that Grier and other "killer dames," as she calls them, want respectability and upward mobility like everyone else. Molly Haskell, "Here Come the Killer Dames," *New York*, May 19, 1975, p. 47.

12. Mark Jacobson, "Sex Goddess of the Seventies," *New York*, May 19, 1975, p. 43.

13. Meehan, *Ladies of the Evening*, p. 109.

14. January 24, 1967, NBC telecast of "The Girl from U.N.C.L.E."

15. Tim Brooks and Earle Marsh, *The Complete Directory of Prime Time Network TV Shows, 1946-Present* (New York: Ballantine Books, 1979, p. 411.

16. "TV's Super Women," *Time*, November 22, 1976, pp. 67–71.

17. Ronald Lackmann, "Lynda Carter," *TV Super Stars '78* (Westport, Conn.: Xerox Education Publishers, 1977), p. 103.

8

Where You Lead, I Will Follow: Women in Pop Music

Women singers convey images through the lyrics they sing and the personal image they project. In live performances, especially, they embody one of the dominant images, Eve, Mary, or independent woman, either in its purity or in some hybrid form. Each musical style—folk, gospel, the blues, musical comedy, or rock and roll—has its own rules that give it its distinctiveness. A gospel singer, for example, cannot sing of pursuing carnal love, and she cannot gyrate across the stage. The bawdy woman singer can do both. Women singers dominate ballad singing and the blues and are well represented in musical comedy, folk, and gospel singing. They are, however, still underrepresented in rock and roll. In all of these mediums, the women specialize in love songs: love of man or love of God. They may whisper or belt a romantic song, as the sound and rhythm may vary, but the lyrics do not.

The instruments of popular music and the performers are influenced by, if not determined by, larger cultural attitudes and values. In Western society, and particularly the United States, machinery is identified with males. Men are considered the inventors and the users of complex machines; this includes electronic musical instruments. It is no accident, therefore, that, with the advent of electronic music, men dominated the field. Combine this with the openly sexual movements of the performers and the explicitly sexual content of the song lyrics, and it is clear why men continue to dominate rock music. As pop music critic Jay Cocks wrote, "Rock is still a kind of music—and a lifestyle—in which women are frequently called 'chicks' and are, as performers or presences, expected to behave accordingly."[1] The few women who have succeeded in the field have been given the dubious distinctions of sounding and acting like men, or in some cases, like black women singers, another outsider group. Janis Joplin, for example, cursed on stage, discussed intimate sexual longings in public, and gyrated with the best of the male performers. In so doing, she became accepted into the male club.

Lyrics can be categorized into three types: traditional (Mary and Eve images), transitional, and assertive (independent woman). The traditional lyrics spoke of woman's devotion to, and determination by, love, her commitment to her lover, her anguish over her lost lover, and her ardent desire to recapture her lover ("Stand By Your Man"). A woman's adult life was shaped by her lover in these songs; this was her occupying and preoccupying concern. The very same theme, of course, was played out in traditional romantic novels, movies, and television melodramas. Transitional lyrics described woman's tentative move away from this obsessive theme. The singer questioned her total devotion to love and lover, wondered about alternative possibilities, and mildly considered separating herself from her lover. Assertive lyrics, rather new on the popular musical scene, openly declared the independence of women. Helen Reddy's "I Am Woman," a popular song of the 1970s, was one of the most famous examples of this point of view. Barbra Streisand's "My Heart Belongs to Me" was another.

Further, women singers projected a public image of themselves while singing; to complicate matters, however, the singer might turn the lyrics around and sing them mockingly or satirically. Billie Holiday, a great blues singer, often satirized the sentiments she expressed. Streisand turned a traditional lament into an assertive cry. But most singers, most of the time, let the words convey the mood and create the meaning. As singers became identified with one musical style and expert at one kind of song, their image was established. In this sense, there is a real similarity between women singers and actresses. Both built careers on one consistent image and became linked to it. During the course of a long career, a singer or actress might change her image, but her popularity was usually associated with her clear definition of an image. And in music, it is attitudes toward romance that pervaded popular songs.

Changing times, though, affected musical styles and messages. In the 1960s, folk singing enjoyed a brief renaissance with such singers as Joan Baez and Judy Collins singing the traditional folk songs as well as antiwar lyrics. Popular music displayed its sex-segregated manner: men monopolized the electric music while women played the single banjo or guitar; men sang aggressively while women sweetly proclaimed the joys or the frustrations of love. In the late 1960s and 1970s, female singers and composers, touched by the women's liberation movement, asserted themselves in new and unprecedented ways. Janis Joplin, for example, sang a song in which she claimed the the right to treat men cruelly. Holly Near wrote and sang explicitly feminist songs such as "It's More Important to Me" and "Strong," songs that told women to be independent and not to compete for men's attention. Dory Previn sang "When a Man Wants a Woman" in which the concluding lines suggested that women doing the same thing would be called predators.

Melanie wrote "Mama, Mama,"a transitional song, in which she complained to her mother that she did not know where she belonged. The accepted roles and patterns no longer seemed acceptable or desirable, but the alternatives were not clear either. Indeed, the women writing songs and singing pop songs in the late 1970s and early 1980s often reflected this confusion. Some remained true to the traditional lyrics, while others reached for a new image and point of view. Still others proclaimed their commitment to the new feminism. Joni Mitchell wrote and sang songs that can be labelled transitional, though openly defiant. Some of her songs expressed the need for self-identity, while others displayed uncertainty about what new identity could be. Barbra Streisand continued to sing traditional, transitional, and assertive songs. "Lullaby to Myself," one of her more recent songs, expressed a contemporary woman's feelings. On her album, *A Star is Born*, Streisand sang "The Woman in the Moon," in which she described a 13-year-old girl who had been told not to act "too strong"; but then, things were changing, she sang, thanks to the woman in the moon. Carole King introduced "Where You Lead" in the early 1970s, a very traditional song, but moved beyond that view at the end of the decade. Carly Simon's "Haven't Got Time for the Pain" showed a woman in transition, impatient with the old ways and searching for the new.

Women in popular music, as writers and performers, shared the same characteristics as women in other parts of popular culture. No one could escape the overarching value system of the culture. The songs describing the new, assertive woman offered only tentative suggestions and solutions to women's divided self, just as social feminists presented equally tentative ideas for women's lives. In this case, there was both a reflective and innovative quality to women's lyrics; they demonstrated the cultural confusion and doubt about the direction of contemporary women while leading to a more self-confident, independent pose, wherever it might lead. A very selective survey of the major types of popular music with a look at some of the great performers offer illustrations of how the lyrics, the style, and the singer portrayed a distinctive image of woman.

Black blues singers emerged in the early twentieth century as popular and powerful celebrities. They were urban, secular singers who turned their rich experiences into social lessons for their audiences. They were usually bolder than white women singers. Performing before exclusively black audiences, they discussed sexual disappointments and the failures of love with great candor. Ida Cox, the "Uncrowned Queen of the Blues," and Ma Rainey, the "Mother of the Blues," established the style that would be used, with spectacular success, by Bessie Smith, the "Empress of the Blues."

Smith was born in Chattanooga, Tennessee, and grew up in poverty. Untrained, she just began singing and at the age of 19, joined a traveling tent show to get out of Chattanooga.[2] She wrote most of the lyrics of her songs and eventually formed her own musical troupe. In 1923 she made her first recording for Columbia Records, "Tain't Nobody's Business If I Do." The double meaning of the words and the silky voice of the singer made the record a big hit. Her second record, "Down Hearted Blues," sold 780,000 copies in less than six months. Although the song was ostensibly a lament, she asserted that she had control of her world. Another hit song was called "You Gotta Give Me Some."

The blues sung by Bessie Smith could be sad or self-mocking, self-indulgent or assertive. Smith was a large woman, five feet nine inches tall and weighing over 200 pounds, but she moved gracefully across a stage. She was known to be hard drinking, frequently unhappy over her failed love affairs, and sometimes violent. In fact, her personal life, known to her fans, was often the source for her new songs. Music historian Donald Bogle noted that Smith "hit anybody who annoyed her or messed with her man or woman."[3] In the mid–1920s, at the height of her career, she earned $2,500 a week touring the black nightclubs of the South. From 1923 to 1929, her records sold between 5 and 10 million copies. Smith's interpretation of lyrics was dramatically effective, and the sound of her voice, smooth, melodic, and strong, made her a very popular entertainer.

A *Time* magazine writer later described Bessie Smith's interpretation of the blues as "a womanly wail that somehow remained proud of its woe."[4] The word "blues" appeared in the title of many of her songs: "Graveyard Dream Blues," "Any Woman's Blues," "Work House Blues," "St. Louis Blues," "Empty Bed Blues," and "House Rent Blues." But as she sang of empty bed blues, she also smiled at the woman's inevitable need for the irresponsible male and mused at the pleasures of sleeping alone occasionally. In the early 1930s, the records of Smith lost their popularity and her career waned. Things began improving a few years later, only to be ended tragically when she was killed in a car accident in 1937 near Clarksdale, Mississippi.

Gospel singer Mahalia Jackson (1911–72) admired the singing style of Bessie Smith. She sang full voiced, belting out her gospel songs in the same fashion as Bessie Smith sang the blues. But Jackson distinguished between gospel singing and blues:

Blues are the songs of despair. . . . Gospel songs are the songs of hope. When you sing gospel you have a feeling there's a cure for what is wrong. When you're through with the blues you've got nothing to rest on.[5]

Bessie Smith probably would disagree with this assessment, but she would have respected Jackson's alternative vision.

Women singers in the United States have shone in musical comedy theater, a popular art form. The Broadway musical always featured women in love, singing their hearts out. Men sang of love as well: Victor Herbert's *Naughty Marietta* (1910), an early example of operetta, introduced "Ah Sweet Mystery of Life," a sentiment that dominated romantic ballads. Among the most popular women singers in Broadway musicals were Gertrude Lawrence, Ethel Merman, and Mary Martin. Music historian Ethan Mordden said that Lawrence was "for some the most appealing star that musical comedy produced."[6]

Gertrude Lawrence (1898–1952) was born in London and made her U.S. debut in 1924. She was a tall, statuesque woman who projected an image of high style, wit, and verve. She gained a large following in New York during the 1930s and 1940s. The critics found her versatile and animated; she could do drawing room comedy as well as musical comedy. Indeed, as critic John Mason Brown noted: "Miss Lawrence was a musical–comedy performer who, though she grew into an admirable actress, had gifts which the legitimate theater could not release. For the full freeing of her powers she needed the singing, dancing, color, and direct communication with an audience made possible by the poster–like values of a musical."[7] Lawrence played Eliza Doolittle in *Pygmalion*, Amanda Prynne in *Private Lives*, and Susan in *Susan and God*, all plays that showed her dramatic talent, while her musical skills were amply demonstrated in *Lady in the Dark* and *The King and I*.

Cole Porter called Ethel Merman's bombastic singing style "the missing link between Lily Pons and Mae West."[8] Born in the Astoria section of New York City on January 16, 1909, Merman first appeared in cabarets and vaudeville before she came to the stage in 1930. She quickly established a reputation as a high energy performer who asserted the woman's right to an opinion and to her freedom. In one of her first great successes, as Reno Sweeney in *Anything Goes* (1934), Merman sang "I Get a Kick Out of You."[9]

The similarity between Merman and Mae West is more than coincidental. As one critic said, "No traveling salesman could fail to understand what Miss Merman may have on her mind."[10] She sang aggressively of a woman's right to love, to initiate sexual encounters, and to compete equally with men. In *Annie Get Your Gun* (1946), Merman played cowgirl Annie Oakley who could shoot a gun to rival Wild Bill Hickok. Romance, of course, also entered into the scenario; Merman acknowledged, in one of the show's many popular songs, "You Can't Get a Man With a Gun," but during the course of the play, she also reminded Bill that "Anything You Can Do, I Can Do Better."[11]

Ethel Merman dominated the Broadway musical stage for over 30 years. As another critic commented: "Even before the atomic bomb, there was Ethel Merman. She may never have flattened a playhouse but she has always shaken the rafters and laid an audience low."[12] Another added, "Her personality is pure Benzedrine."[13] Merman's inimitable style kept bringing the fans into the theater. She was an Eve and independent woman combined. Her predictable image, in musical after musical, apparently pleased her following. Among her other credits was a portrayal of Rose in *Gypsy* in 1959 for which she won the New York Drama Critics Award for best female lead in a musical and her rendering of Dolly Gallagher in *Hello Dolly!*

Ethel Merman's personality lent itself, of course, to her spirited defense of womanhood. Her sheer ebullience could not be contained in a role that did not have both Eve-like and independent woman qualities. She was a large woman, closer to Mae West and Sophie Tucker's physique, than to that of Gertrude Lawrence. "To her," commented a critic, "though abundant fun, s-e-x is obviously a laughing matter at which she laughs as heartily as she succeeds in making the rest of us."[14] The similarity to the bawdy women entertainers is apparent. Because she did not have the physical makeup or the personality to be a sweet, demure Mary nor the angular sexual figure of an Eve or independent woman, she satirized the images, took the offensive, and parodied the forbidden subject. In so doing, she made herself into an independent Eve in much the same way that Mae West and Sophie Tucker did. But she did it on the popular musical comedy stage where the suggestiveness replaced open acknowledgment of the topic.

If Ethel Merman projected the independent Eve image, sure and self-confident, Mary Martin came closer to the sweet Mary who could, and would, assert her spunk and sexiness on occasion. She sang the teasing "My Heart Belongs to Daddy," in the 1938 production of *Leave It To Me* and she played *Peter Pan* in 1954. She could combine her sweet reasonableness with determination, as she showed in the 1949 production of *South Pacific* where, as nurse Nellie Forbush, Martin promised "I'm Gonna Wash That Man Right Outa My Hair," but later had second thoughts.[15] Born in Weatherford, Texas, on December 11, 1913, her family moved to Nashville where she grew up. She studied to be a singer and first appeared at the Trocadero Night Club in Hollywood. Her credits included *One Touch of Venus* and on tour *Annie Get Your Gun* (1947–48). Both Martin and Merman played in *Hello, Dolly!* and *Annie, Get Your Gun* on Broadway.[16]

Two of the greatest hits of Mary Martin were *South Pacific* and *Peter Pan*. Her portrayals of the brave nurse Nellie Forbush and the eternally optimistic

Peter Pan projected an image of certainty within an essential sincerity and homespun nature. Mary Martin convinced her audience that she was a traditional woman who had to assume unusual roles during unusual times. Another success was her portrayal of Maria Von Trapp in *The Sound of Music*, a role she originated in 1959. She won the New York Drama Critics' Award for this as well. The popular singer-actress Julie Andrews later played the role in the movies. Indeed, Andrews is a worthy successor to Mary Martin; she shared many of the same personality traits—a sweet charm that harmonized with a strong will.

The Broadway theater and the musical comedy stages around the country never attracted the numbers of people that a successful movie, novel, or television program did, but through recordings the music and the character of the female musical stars could be appreciated. Simultaneous with other musical forms, the musical comedy expressed the very same romantic themes. While Katharine Hepburn displayed courage and independence in her films of the 1930s and 1940s, so Ethel Merman and Mary Martin sang out similar messages on Broadway. Crossing popular cultural lines, talented singers linked hands with talented actresses.

In contemporary music, the rock and roll woman singer inherited the mantle of the blues singer. She is a sturdy but minor player in a heavily dominated male field. The rock singer accelerated the musical rhythm and the sound, turned the blues into an aggressive scream, and replaced passivity with action. She was still concerned with love lost, but she was an active player in the game. Tina Turner best exemplifies a successful woman rocker. She has received the ultimate compliment from rock cognoscenti by being called the female Mick Jagger. She was born Anna Mae Bullock in Nutbush, a country town near Brownsville, Tennessee, in 1940. Like her older sister Eileen, and her parents, Floyd and Zelma Bullock, she picked cotton and strawberries on the land her father managed for a white plantation boss. Turner began singing as a teenager and enjoyed some success in local talent contests. She and her sister frequented a rhythm and blues establishment called the Club Manhattan in East St. Louis, where they then lived. In 1956 she met Ike Turner, who played at that club with his Kings of Rhythm group. Anna Mae became Tina and the lead singer for the Kings of Rhythm.

Ike Turner shaped Tina's image into that of a wild, uninhibited wailer of low-down blues. She contributed a dance that resembled the shimmy and the shake of Mae West and Eva Tanguay. From 1956 to 1976, they built an audience within the black community with their raucous rhythm and blues sound and rambunctious style. By that time, the marriage ended and Tina Turner later said: "I never wanted to do all that moaning, begging and pleading. I always preferred rock to r & b."[17] She began performing rock material in Las Vegas. Hits such as "Let's Stay Together," her single record of 1983, and her album *Private Dancer* established her as a successful practitioner of music usually reserved for male rockers.

Tina Turner has been called the "Mae West of Rock," an accurate description of her robust persona on stage and concrete evidence that the sexually explicit woman singer is connected to the bawdy woman performer. Turner is the independent Eve, living testimony to the vitality of that dominant image in the late 1980s. Her style is also a natural evolution from the mocking blues to the aggressive no-nonsense, rock music of the 1980s. She is part of an old musical tradition as well as representative of a durable image of women.

One brand of folk music, country and western, emerged from its regional roots in the 1960s and 1970s to become nationally known and popular. Dolly Parton is one of country's most successful singers. She has recorded, made movies (most notably *Nine to Five* and *The Best Little Whorehouse in Texas*), and appeared on television. Parton also continues to tour the traditional county fairs and popular concert halls. She has been the recipient of many Country Western Association awards and has had numerorus successful albums. Her distinctive appearance, winning smile, and personal charm has gained her a national following.

Parton shared a similar background with many of the black blues singers. Born in 1946, she was the fourth of 12 children, raised by a struggling dirt farmer and his wife. Growing up in the foothills of the Great Smoky Mountains in Tennessee, she began singing and writing songs before she could read and write. Her maternal grandfather was a minister, and Dolly loved to sing gospel songs in Grandfather Owen's church.[18] As she told one interviewer: "we didn't feel ashamed to sing and play our git-tars. We believed in makin' a joyful noise unto the Lord."[19] Parton has written hundreds of songs, most of which came from her personal experience of growing up in the rural South in a financially poor, but emotionally, warm environment.

After high school, Dolly Parton left her home for Nashville, the capital of country music. She began recording songs and in 1967 was hired by Porter Wagoner, one of country-western's best-known performers, to sing in his band. She sang with him for seven years gaining experience and popularity. In 1974 Parton formed her own band, largely consisting of her own family, and called it the Travelin' Family Band. At this point in her career, she began to gain national media attention. Reporters from national magazines and newspapers covered her concerts and reviewed her albums. *New York Times* critic John Rockwell commented:

She is an impressive artist. . . . Her visual landmark is not far from that of Diamond Lil: a mountainous, curlicued bleached blonde wig, lots of makeup, and outfits that accentuate her quite astonishing hourglass figure. But Miss Parton is no artificial dumb blonde. Her thin little soprano and girlish way of talking suggests something childlike, but one quickly realizes both that it is genuine and that she is a striking talent.[20]

Parton is small, barely five feet tall, with an unusually large bosom for a small woman. Her puffed blonde wigs, combined with her bejeweled and sequined costumes, drew a lot of attention from the critics. As her fame grew, so did the comments on her appearance. While Parton's songs could wryly wonder about man as a faithful lover, her outward appearance suggested a woman who relied upon her physical being to attract that very same man. When asked about this apparent contradiction, Parton responded, "If people think I'm a dumb blonde because of the way I look, then they're dumber than they think I am."[21]

She explained, in numerous interviews, that, as a poor young woman, she never had beautiful clothes or makeup. Now she was a rich, successful woman who was enjoying the fruits of her labor. As long as her costumes and appearance pleased her, she asserted, she would continue to dress that way. While commentators compared her to Mae West and Diamond Lil, viewed her as a glitzy persona, and called her "a playful female impersonator,"[22] Parton blithely and unconcernedly carried on. "If you have talent," she said, "people are gonna overlook it, unless you've got somethin' to get attention."[23] On another occasion she commented: "I am as stubborn as a mule. I have my own idea about who I am, what I am and I am very pleased and content with that."[24]

In the late 1970s, Dolly Parton sang of a "Travelling Man" whom the singer had expected to run away with only to discover that he had left with her mother the night before. In "To Daddy," a daughter sang wryly of her devoted mother who always sacrificed for the family; one morning they all awoke to learn that their mother had left without informing Daddy when, or if, she would return. She continued to sing her earlier popular songs such as "My Tennessee Mountain Home" and "Coat of Many Colors," which described a coat her mother had made her when she was a child. Thus, her songs and her style reflected a combination of traditional folk lyrics and assertive, modern sensitivity to the plight of women.

Dolly Parton conveyed the image of a knowing, shrewd woman who may have loved and lost but who rebuilt herself afterward. She organized a rock band in 1977 called Gypsy Fever and toured the country. As reviewer Jean Vallely of *Time* reported, "A Dolly Parton concert is a treat, like a hot-fudge sundae after a month of dieting."[25] Parton was a sure survivor, an adept adaptor, just like the independent Eves played by Barbara Stanwyck in the movies of the 1930s. In some sense, however, Parton projected an interesting merger of all three images of women. She was called "homespun"by one critic,[26] a quality that blended with her newly acquired worldly ways. Her ample form suggested an Eve, while her grit, determination, and self-confidence surely qualified her as an independent woman. Parton clearly used the gaudy outfits, the bouffant wigs, and the five-inch gold shoes to distinguish herself from other country singers. She sang romantic ballads traditionally and mockingly; she projected humor, self-parody, and social satire. Parton synthesized all three images to create a distinctive persona.

In addition to folk, country, blues, and musical comedy, commercial Tin Pan Alley–produced songs have appealed to the public throughout this century. Writing for vaudeville and burlesque singers, stage, radio, movies, and television singers, commercial songwriters produced some of the country's most popular songs. Most of these writers were men, and they wrote romantic tunes for women singers. Dinah Shore's career was in this field. Shore sang commercial songs in a straightforward manner, appearing as a sweet-natured down-to-earth Mary type. In 1956, already an established star, she told *TV Guide*: "Show business is a man's world. So is everything else, for that matter."[27] This was not said with rancor, but rather acceptance. In the same interview, Shore pointed out that women stars had to retain their femininity to be successful on television; rather than be a leading emcee on her musical variety show, she said, "I stick strictly to being a hostess."[28]

Dinah Shore's songs did not challenge social expectations for women's lives. Her love ballads always affirmed the importance of love, romance, and family. Her obvious sincerity endeared her to two generations of audiences. She had a multifaceted career: Dinah Shore enjoyed success as a nightclub and concert singer, a recording artist, a radio star, and a television personality. Her early career began inauspiciously. Born in Winchester, Tennessee, in 1917, she moved to Nashville with her family when she was six. Shore graduated from Vanderbilt University and then went to New York. In January 1939 she got a job singing with the Leo Reisman Orchestra. The *Variety* reviewer wrote of her performance: "After a short band number, the gal vocalist, Dinah Shore is on for a single number, 'Won't You Hurry Home.' Nicely gowned, sells a song passably, and has an unaffected ease of manner, but doesn't pile up much of a wallop for the windup."[29]

Many of the characteristics noted by the *Variety* critic became the basis for the greatest success of Shore: her "unaffected ease of manner" made her comfortably pleasant to her audiences; her self-assured, yet not bombastic, style appealed to both sexes. Dinah Shore was also well liked by her cohorts. She was known for her cooperative manner, her intelligence, and her willingness to work hard. In September 1940, for example, she went on the *Eddie Cantor Show*, one of the most popular radio shows at the time. Cantor said of her:

You wouldn't believe it, I never knew anybody who worked so hard. Every week she would show up with 20 new songs. She'd rehearse them, she'd learn them and she wanted to sing all 20 to me, so I could pick out one for the show.[30]

Her 1940 recording of "Yes, My Darling Daughter" sold a million copies. During the 1940s, she was second only to Frank Sinatra in popularity. U.S. soldiers overseas also voiced their admiration for her. In 1946 three of her records sold 1 million copies each. She was voted the country's best-known and favorite vocalist for both 1950 and 1951. As late as 1960, she was ranked by the public as the ninth most admired woman in the country.

"Dinah's Open House," her 1944 radio show, continued to keep her in the limelight as did the six movies she made during that period. In 1951, the same year "I Love Lucy" premiered, Shore left radio for television. Twice a week for 15 minutes each time, she sang and had guests who performed. This format remained on the air until 1956 when the "Dinah Shore Chevrolet Show" began. It was an hourlong variety show in which she continued to sing the slogan–commercial that made the Chevy famous: "See the U.S.A. in your Chevrolet." The show remained high in audience ratings for seven seasons.

Dinah Shore left television in 1962 only to return with a new afternoon variety show in 1970. On "Dinah's Place," she cooked, talked to guests, and sang. The informal atmosphere combined with Dinah's easy manner made the show very successful. Some critics complained that Shore smiled all of the time, but most people agreed with television journalist Barbara Walters that Dinah Shore was like "the American flag."[31] The show won the Outstanding Daytime Program Award in 1972 and 1976.[32] Indeed, television, a more intimate medium than the movies, captured the warm personality of Dinah Shore effectively. She called herself an optimist who enjoyed the intimacy of television. The show lasted ten years, qualifying it as one of television's longest runners.

Dinah Shore believed in the equality of women, but she also thought that men and women should have different social roles to perform. Though she had been a working professional during her 19-year marriage to actor George Montgomery, she valued her family life equally. In 1979 she told her biographer Bruce Cassidy that "I was always an emancipated woman," but she was shocked by the militant feminists who came on her talk show and displayed open hostility to men.

I deplore that. It's always been a man's world, and it probably always will be. I don't want to change that. All of my career, on radio, in recording studios, in films and on television, men have made the decisions for me, and they've usually been the right ones.[33]

So 23 years after she expressed the same sentiment to a *TV Guide* reporter, Shore repeated it. Surely her successful career on television owed much to her nonthreatening manner, especially during the sometimes angry days of women's liberation. She got along with men and women and conveyed a placidity that assured many and upset only the few activists who wished to shake her out of her sweetness. But Dinah Shore on afternoon television and Mary Tyler Moore on evening television represented the Mary image in a period when it had minimal exposure in popular culture.

Shore assured the traditionalists that Marys had not been entirely abandoned or lost. Though there is no one quite like Dinah Shore on contemporary television (there are no musical variety shows at all), the image she projected appears to return in other forms. In the 1980s, for instance, popular rock singer Linda Ronstadt changed her image and sang 1940s style romantic ballads reminiscent of Dinah Shore's songs. Barbra Streisand contiued to sing all kinds of different messages and made a hit record album of Broadway musical songs. The traditional romantic ballad continued to be sung alongside the bombastic, assertive rock and roll song. Traditional, transitional, and assertive lyrics and styles coexist in the eclectic 1980s, an apt symbol that all of the basic images of women remain alive and needed.

NOTES

1. Jay Cocks, "Chick Singers Need Not Apply," *Time*, January 21, 1980, p. 81.

2. Biographical information on Bessie Smith can be obtained from a variety of sources. Henry Pleasants, *The Great American Popular Singers* (New York: Simon and Schuster, 1974), has a cogent introduction to her life and work as does Linda Dahl in *Stormy Weather* (New York: Pantheon Books, 1984).

3. Donald Bogle, *Brown Sugar* (New York: Harmony Books, 1980), p. 22.

4. Pleasants, *American Popular Singers*, p. 70.

5. Ibid., p. 199.

6. Ethan Mordden, *Broadway Babies: The People Who Made the American Musical* (New York: Oxford University Press, 1983), p. 108.

7. John Mason Brown, "Blithe Spirit—Gertrude Lawrence," *Saturday Review of Literature*, September 27, 1952, pp. 24–26, and quoted in William C. Young, ed., *Famous Actors and Actresses on the American Stage: Documents of American Theater History*, vo. 2 (New York: R. R. Bowker, 1975), p. 669.

8. Mordden, *Broadway Babies*, p. 115.

9. Young, *Actors and Actresses*, pp. 784–89.

10. Ibid., p. 787.

11. Ibid., pp. 785–89.

12. Ibid., p. 785.

13. Ibid., p. 787.

14. Ibid.

15. Ian Herbert, et al., ed., *Who's Who in the Theatre*, vol. 2 (Detroit: Gale Research, 1981).

16. Ibid.

17. Cathleen McGuigan, "The Second Coming of Tina," *Newsweek*, September 10, 1984, p. 76.

18. There are many popular articles on Parton. For biographical information, *Current Biography 1977* (New York: H. W. Wilson Co.) is reliable, pp. 338–41, as is Alanna Nash, *Dolly* (Los Angeles: Reed Books, 1978).

19. Quoted in *Current Biography 1977*.

20. John Rockwell, "Songs Presented by Dolly Parton," *New York Times*, September 16, 1974, p. 43.

21. Margo Jefferson, "Dolly Parton: bewigged, bespangled . . . and proud," *Ms.*, June 1979, p. 16.

22. Ibid.

23. Jack Hurst, "You've come a long way, Dolly," *High Fidelity*, December 1977, p. 122.

24. Nash, *Dolly*, p. 197.

25. Jean Vallely, "On the rock road with Dolly Parton," *Time*, April 18, 1977, p. 72.

26. Roy Blount, Jr., "Country's angels," *Esquire*, March 1977, p. 126.

27. Dinah Shore," *TV Guide*, December 15, 1956, p. 13.

28. Ibid.

29. Quoted in Bruce Cassidy, *Dinah! A Biography* (New York: Franklin Watts, 1979), p. 29.

30. Ibid., p. 39.

31. Ibid., p. 212.

32. Sandra Lee Stuart, *Who Won What When: The Book of Winners* (New York: Lyle Stuart, 1977), p. 75.

33. Ibid., p. 166.

9

Women in Sports

Although the U.S. cultural imagination has been able to visualize a variety of independent women types, it has had the greatest difficulty imagining women athletes. Indeed, in order to make this new phenomenon acceptable to most of the public, especially in the twentieth century, the media have defined these women within the three dominant images. The talent, skill, and accomplishment have been assumed and subsumed. Makers of popular culture presented these women to the public as sweet, young Marys, seductive Eves, or spunky independent women. First, however, trend setters had to overcome a number of cultural prejudices.

Physical activity, strenuous exercise, and sweating were not, and still are not, associated with the female gender. Nor were the physical traits of strength, endurance, and agility. Further, the cultural goals of discipline, group play, and especially competition were deemed inappropriate for women. If anyone needed further convincing, especially during the last century, they were reminded that adult women lived in the domestic sphere, away from competition and hurly-burly groups. Young girls were not preparing for adult lives of athletic competition, nor did they require training in group cooperation. They learned what they needed to know from their mothers. Biology and culture, then, united to discourage women from engaging in sports.

Athletic activity could be positively harmful to a young woman's adolescent body, or so thought doctors, preachers, and teachers throughout the nineteenth century. Fear of injury to female reproductive organs was also regularly expressed as a reason for denying young women athletic opportunities.[1] Women were delicate flowers, sweet Marys, prone to sickness and weakness. Advocates of physical education for women countered these arguments by noting that women endured pain in childbirth, were used to strenuous work, and could overcome their frailties, precisely by training their bodies through physical activity. The detractors, however, outnumbered the supporters. Though physical education classes for young women began in the last century, they were modest affairs.

Many young women, however, enjoyed running, playing ball, and developing their skills on the playing fields. And they found men and women teachers and coaches who supported their wishes. It is in school, after all, that children learn athletic skills and the rules of the games. If young women had no supporters there, they were in trouble. Another factor that helped the supporters of women athletes was the popularity of the bicycle in the late nineteenth century; both sexes loved it and conservative doubters had to keep revising their reasons for denying women the right to ride. In high schools and the new colleges for women in the 1870s and 1880s, physical education classes were inaugurated. Though always fighting an uphill battle, both individual and team sports grew.

One of the preoccupying concerns of the advocates was how to design athletic programs for women that avoided the negative aspects of the men's programs, particularly, the ugly competitive spirit that seemed to pervade men's athletics. As Lucille Eaton Hill, director of physical training at Wellesley College said in 1903, "We must avoid the evils which are so apparent to thoughtful people in the conduct of athletics for men." Senda Berenson, the originator of women's basketball in the 1890s and athletic director at Smith College, was particularly worried: "The greatest element of evil in the spirit of athletics in this country is the idea that one must win at any cost—that defeat is an unspeakable disgrace."[2]

Berenson created women's basketball rules in such a way as to satisfy her own qualms as well as those of the conservatives. Indeed, the solution she provided became the model for women's team sports until recent times. The rules she promulgated were less strenuous (so as not to exert the young women unduly), (less competitive to reduce the chances of injury), and confined to intramural activity (to discourage even more competition). Intercollegiate athletics for women was not allowed; instead, women's colleges had play days, where women from other schools joined together informally to play, not to compete.

The rules devised by Berenson for women's basketball harmonized with dominant cultural values: a player could not take the ball away from the holder; each player was confined to one (or later two) areas of play; the ball could be held for three seconds only (later modified to allow three bounces).[3] The game was to be ladylike, played by young Marys with no independent women or, perish the thought, Eves around. It was to satisfy contradictory claims simultaneously. While women engaged in athletics, they were required to behave in a feminine fashion. This compromise, or uneasy synthesis, satisfied some, but not all players and teachers. It created a new social type: the female athlete, the woman who engaged in strenuous athletic activity while retaining her delicate femininity.

Many women's colleges, however, ignored the rules of Berenson and played by the men's rules. A few schools participated in intercollegiate competition.[4] Among the Seven Sisters (the prestigious women's colleges in the Northeast), Smith became known for its women's athletic program and was described by some as having women who were "all health and normality" in contrast to the brainy girls at Bryn Mawr and the radical types at Vassar.[5] Apparently, Smith athletes had found the proper way to act out the new role of female athlete and presented themselves as normal, conventional women. They did not aspire to professional sports, nor did they carry their athletic enthusiasm to extravagant heights.

Ladylike sportswomen appeared in all of the other sports as well. Defenders of women in sports sometimes shared part of the culturally conservative views; while they believed women had the right to be athletic, they did not want them to exert themselves too much. They maintained that, while sports may not harm a woman's body, they should be practiced in such a way as to insure that fact. Women should not engage in masculine sports such as wrestling, boxing, or football. Finally, when women entered team sports, not only should they not compete with other women's teams, but they should never dream of playing with, or against, men's teams. They must remain soft in appearance and behavior at all costs.

Prejudice grows out of, or at least is fostered by, cultural attitudes, but in the case of women there are physiological considerations as well, although the considerations once frequently cited, primarily menstruation, parturition, lactation, and fear of injury to reproductive organs and breasts, are now recognized to be not as inhibiting as previously believed. It is now generally believed that "the normal healthy female may participate in any athletic endeavor for which her training and experience prepare her."[6]

The above statement was written in 1981, not 1881, and though the author acknowledged that recent medical opinion believed that women were capable of any, and all, athletic training, the qualified way the statement was written ("now recognized to be not as inhibiting") suggested the author still had his doubts. Overcoming long-held views on the subject of women in sports was difficult to do. Allen Guttman, in his survey of modern sports, noted that "the exclusion of women from sports . . . has lasted longer than the exclusion of blacks."[7] Further, women athletes, until the 1960s and 1970s, accepted the cultural boundaries set for them. They rarely rocked the boat or challeged the conventional wisdom. Gratefully, they played as college students, and later possibly as amateurs, and only rarely as professionals. Most suppressed any ambition they may have had to become a professional and to distinguish themselves in athletics.

The gradual acceptance of women in sports began, prior to the 1970s, by seeing women participate in individual (not team), and amateur (not professional), sporting events. A very selective survey of women's sports over time supports these generalizations. Although team sports for men are very popular in the United States, they have never achieved a similar status for women. There are amateur and professional women's basketball and baseball teams, for example, but their popularity has remained local or at best regional. It is in golf, tennis, skating, and track that women attained standing, success, and some recognition. However, the essential cultural message underpinned the structure of even the sports where women made a niche for themselves.

The emergence of women athletes coincided with the rise of popular newspapers and magazines; as a result, writers who reported on their doings tended to depict the women according to their physical appearance and the personality they projected. Consciously or unconsciously, they adopted the basic imagery used in popular literature and later in the movies and television to describe women athletes. To gain a following for their coverage, they had to define a clear and simple portrait, one not too complex or ambiguous. Women athletes, then, became real-life figures who took on the same images usually associated with screen roles or television parts. While there was some separation between a movie star and her movies, the woman athlete became the real and mythic character all rolled into one.

The first woman athlete who became a great media favorite was Babe Didrikson Zaharias. Born to Norwegian immigrants in Port Arthur, Texas, in 1912, Babe (she had been called Baby as a child and, in deference to Babe Ruth, she shortened it to Babe) was a natural, all-around athlete. She played baseball and basketball and participated in track events. In her senior year of high school, she played in an interdistrict game that led to her playing for one of the best girls' basketball teams in the country, the Golden Cyclone Athletic Club of the Employers Casualty Company of Dallas. Her story already sounds amazingly like the biography of a budding film star.

Her extraordinary athletic talents were already noticed by the newspapers. In an article with her byline for the *New York Times* before the 1932 Olympics, she told the readers: "Naturally athletics have not left me much time for household tasks for which a girl is supposed to have some liking, but I do not care about them. If necessary, however, I can sew and cook."[8] She broke three women's world records at the Los Angeles Olympics; Babe threw the javelin, high jumped, and did the 80-meter hurdle better than anyone had ever done before. Her throwing arm awed observers; she threw a completed pass of 47 yards and could throw a baseball 313 feet from centerfield to the plate.

She quickly became a much-covered personality. Her straightforward, plain-talking ways appealed to the public. Her behavior also elicited attention. She endorsed an automobile company, which led to her suspension from the Amateur Athletic Union. Though they had second thoughts and were willing to reinstate her, Babe decided to become a professional. This was the first of many run-ins with the amateur association. Her ambitions to perform and to be rewarded for her efforts conflicted with the women's amateur association's view of female athletes. The Texan facing off against the big-city Eastern players became a motif in her press coverage.

At that point in her career, Babe Didrikson decided to capitalize on her success and growing fame. She barnstormed in a vaudeville act of her own, touring small towns throughout the country. She putted shots, did acrobatics, and played the mouth organ. She told one interviewer in 1944 that she had earned a substantial amount of money during the Great Depression and was able to support her family and take time off to practice the one sport she had not yet mastered—golf. In her first golf tournament in October 1934, she had a card of 92. In April 1935 she won the Texas Women's Golf Association Championship, but not before receiving criticism from some of the amateur women golfers. Their public remarks reflected their concern for a proven winner, but also displayed other, usually unspoken attitudes. Peggy Chandler, a tournament finalist, declared: "We really don't need any truck driver's daughter in this tournament," and others called Babe "too manly, too muscular to engage in competition with their frail ilk."[9] The image projected by the reporters as well as the golfers she competed against was of a manly Babe, a woman who defied the ladylike image usually associated with amateur golf. Sweet Mary types, apparently, were the only suitable women golfers.

The United States Golf Association refused to let her play as an amateur so she turned pro for the second time; there would be yet a third time that she would conflict with the association. She toured with the leading male golfer of the day, Gene Sarazen, and told one interviewer in June 1936 that "It's a sort of a lonely business, being a woman pro. There is no Women's Open or Pro Championships to play in."[10] After winning more tournaments, she decided to return to amateur status to be able to play in a continuous series of tournaments.

In December 1938 she married wrestler George Zaharias. He became her greatest supporter and constant companion. After winning the Women's Western Open in both 1944 and 1945, she became the first woman to have won that tournament three times. The Associated Press poll of sportswriters voted her the Woman Athlete of 1945 and 1946. Babe Didrickson Zaharias had, by that point, won a substantial following. Her naturally gregarious nature and her pleasant bantering on the golf course made her a favorite. As one columnist remarked:

She will outdraw the big majority of our male heroes and pull a gallery of twenty-five hundred any old time. . . . Playing from women's tees, she will equal men's par 60 per cent of the time. . . . Babe is the first woman golfer to pay any attention to showmanship. She will josh her rivals and kid with the gallery—and how the spectators love that sort of thing.[11]

Golf was becoming a very popular sport for women, and the professionals wanted more opportunities to play. In 1946 the first professional tour was organized, but problems soon developed. Three years later, Zaharias's manager, Fred Corcoran, organized the Ladies Professional Golf Association and began a tour that included four stops with a purse of $15,000 and a bonus of $5,000 to the winner. In 1948, and again in 1950 and 1954, Babe won the U.S. Women's Open, the major tournament on the pro circuit. In 1953 she discovered that she had cancer and underwent surgery. The national press followed her recovery and her return to golf. She won five tournaments in 1954, satisfying the great hopes of the media and the public for her recovery; the following year she won two more tournaments but succumbed to cancer in 1956.

As one experienced observer noted after her death:

The untimely passing of the Babe robbed the golfing world of one of its most dynamic personalities and was a distinct, if temporary, setback to the women's tour. The Babe was not merely a prodigious hitter, a player who often brought off the impossible recovery, and one who amazed everyone with her delicate touch around the greens; she was also a showman through and through. She loved the limelight, and she entertained her audience to the full. . . . The Babe was the most promotable commodity women's golf has ever known.[12]

Babe Didrikson Zaharias became a major celebrity as a woman athlete. Although many sports writers characterized her as "Muscle Moll" and "muscle woman," descriptive terms she resented mightily, others noted that she carried her five foot, six inch, 145 pound figure very gracefully.[13] Reporters protrayed her as a female Samson, a woman whose physique resembled that of a man more than a woman. Therefore, she was hard to categorize; she was too serious, too determined, and too competitive to qualify as the average female athlete. However, her winning personality as well as her awesome athleticism impressed all observers. Because she was a new phenomenon, the popular culture writers followed her avidly. Generally, they emphasized her extraordinary accomplishments, focusing upon her records, those she made and those she broke. She was an outstanding athlete, an incredible woman athlete, and thus an exception, not the future rule for women in sports.

It is clear, though, that she opened up new avenues of opportunity for women in golf. Babe became the first woman to be offered a head professional job at a golf club, one of the first to become a successful professional, and the first to insist on substantial purses for women players. Because of her popularity, she brought attention to the women's golf tour and gave the sport respect, national attention, and commercial possibilities. But, as much as she did, the Babe was not able to change the public view that women pros were rare flowers, unlike the natural place held by male pros in the public mind.

While one of her contemporaries, Patty Berg, became a national favorite as well, she was portrayed as the sweet young thing, the girl-woman golfer. Few professionals attained the fame of Babe Didrikson Zaharias. Her success owed much to great talent, her charismatic personality, and her ability to use the newspapers, newsreels, and magazines to her advantage. The press saw her as a female version of Will Rogers, a blunt-speaking Texan going up against the genteel snobbism of country club golfers. She became Every-woman in a nation wracked by the depression, a woman who had risen from the ranks, through her own efforts, talent, and hard work, a true American dream story.

Female professional golfers continue to receive smaller purses than male golfers and receive less publicity during their tournaments. In the 1930s, 1940s, and 1950s, sports-minded readers, even if they were not particularly interested in golfing, knew of the Babe. That cannot be said of any contemporary woman golfer. There are no female equivalents of Arnold Palmer or Jack Nicklaus.

Tennis today has become a very popular spectator and participant sport. Women have been playing tennis in this country since the 1880s. The first women's single championship was held in Philadelphia in 1887. Women tennis players were amateurs for the most part, and those who became professionals were given less prize money than the men. This situation did not change until the 1970s. Tennis for both men and women pretended to be an amateur sport long after that was the reality. As one expert noted, "The best players were pros, but the best tournaments were amateur."[14] Since tennis began as an elite sport, its amateur status was prized; it was socially improper to be paid for a leisure time activity. Snobbism and elitism characterized tennis and golf. They were both upper-class sports initially.

It is perhaps more than coincidental that the women responsibile for opening up both sports to more women were lower-middle-class women: Babe Zaharias and Billie Jean King both came from modest family backgrounds. They both sought public recognition and financial reward. Neither was too polite to let anyone and everyone know that fact. Talented upper-class women athletes, presumably, were trained to tame their talent, restrain their ambition, and mute their voices. This was not the case for striving women who knew financial hardships and who yearned for recognition and acknowledgment of their talent.

Tennis, like golf, had its media coverage. Helen Wills Moody, for example, considered by many to be the greatest woman tennis player ever, was well known to her contemporaries earlier in the century, though she was not considered a favorite with the gallery. She was very serious, earnest, and singleminded while playing. But as one reporter observed, "Of course, there is no reason why an amateur athlete should try to please galleries."[15] While Moody was called "Little Miss Poker Face," Billie Jean King became the fiery feminist, the spunky critic of the genteel rules of tennis that excluded women from equal treatment.

King, born in Long Beach, California in 1943, began playing tennis as a very young child. She won her first championship at Wimbledon, England, one of the most prestigious titles in the world of tennis. In her most recent autobiography (she has written two), King discussed how and why she became a tennis player. She described how she had loved to play baseball with her brother Randy, who went on to become a professional baseball player. But she discovered that, as a girl striving to succeed in a distinctly male sport, she had no chance. "There is no life for girls in team sports past Little League." This awareness made her think about which sport to enter.

I got into tennis when I realized this, and because I thought golf would be too slow for me, and I was too scared to swim. What else could a little girl do if she wasn't afraid to sweat? But as good as I was, and as much as I loved tennis right from the start, I found myself out of place there, too, because it was a country-club game then, and I came from a working-class family. My father was a fireman, and we didn't have any money for rackets, much less for proper tennis dresses.[16]

King went on to recount how she was not allowed to pose in a group photograph at the Los Angeles Tennis Club during the Southern California Junior Championships because she was wearing a blouse and shorts rather than the official, ladylike tennis dress. None of these obstacles, of course, stopped Billie Jean King from becoming a champion. She brought a new style to women's tennis by playing a fast-paced net game, in contrast to the old-time greats like Moody who stayed in the back court. King's agility at the net, her clear talents as an all-around athlete, and her quick wit and temper attracted a great deal of attention.

Billie Jean King became the independent woman of tennis. She was the Katharine Hepburn of her sport, articulate, aggressive, and nonapologetic; she recognized her own skills, expected others to acknowledge them, and also expected the profession to reward her accordingly. She was a shining example of the new feminism of the modern era. She anticipated many of the themes of the women's movement of the 1970s. The media found her to be an attractive and salable representative of the new woman athlete. Babe Didrikson, by contrast, did not have a feminist perspective, nor did she have a public women's movement to support her; she appeared as a lone spokeswoman.

As early as 1967, King insisted that the goal for women tennis players was equal prize money, an equal number of worthy tournaments, and the same respect granted to male players. She was a dramatic contrast to previous greats in women's tennis. The grand old lady of the game, Hazel Hotchkiss Wightman (1886–1974), for example, told reporters in the last year of her life: "Back in 1906, I was offered $300 to play an exhibition. I refused it. I couldn't imagine why anyone would want to pay me, anyway."[17] King challenged that view, and with the help of lots of television coverage, told the public why women athletes of talent and accomplishment deserved equal rewards with men. Television, indeed, played a major role in her career advancement and in publicizing women's tennis.

During the course of her impressive career, King not only got herself into the record book, but she scored major victories for women's tennis. In 1970 she and tennis magazine publisher Gladys Heldman, began the Virginia Slims tournament, the first major professional tour for women. Thanks to their efforts, women tennis pros were assured of a yearlong tour of play, with substantial prize money. They also began a new magazine called *womanSport* to feature women athletes. In 1971 Billie Jean King won $117,000 in the Slims tournament, the first woman athlete to earn over $100,000 in prize money in one year. Since earnings have always been a measure of success in professional sports, King's accomplishment became newsworthy.

In 1973, while Australian Margaret Court lost to former Wimbledon star Bobby Riggs on Mother's Day, Billie Jean King beat him 6–4, 6–3, 6–3 on September 1 of that year. The televised King-Riggs match drew a large audience as well as a live audience of over 30,000 to the Houston Astrodome. Though criticized by some as an overdone show business event, the tennis match became a symbol for many female athletes that women's sporting activities had gained respect. As Curry Kirkpatrick wrote in *Sports Illustrated*:

Because of Billie Jean alone, who was representing a sex supposedly unequipped for such things, what began as a huckster's hustle in defiance of serious athleticism ended up not mocking the game of tennis but honoring it. This night King was both a shining piece of show biz and the essence of what sport is all about.[18]

While no one, including King, seriously believed, that women tennis players could compete against men of their own age and talent, the King-Riggs match took on another meaning: it gave authenticity to women athletes.

According to Bud Collins, it was one of the two televised events that made tennis a national sport with a national audience.[19]

Though King recognized that support from the women's movement was essential to her success, she considered herself an individualist and was uncomfortable with any label. In 1974 she wrote, "When it comes to Women's Lib, I am pretty much of a pragmatist, and I'd bet that most other women are too."[20] Her goal, she consistently maintained, was to remove all labels from members of both sexes. At the same time, she acknowledged that she and all female athletes benefited from the organized women's movement. She actively developed women's coalitions to cooperate with her in her reform efforts, and she became a familiar face on television as both a player and commentator. She testified before congressional committees as to why young girls should receive physical education and why the government should insure equal funding for women's athletic programs.

Another example of King's innovative approach to tennis was her participation in the creation of World Team Tennis in 1974. This league lasted only four years, but it provided another model for professional tennis players: men and women playing on the same team. King became the player-coach of the Philadelphia Freedoms, the first woman in charge of a team with male professional athletes. She later played for the New York Apples. Unfortunately, the concept did not win with the fans, and while the Virginia Slims tournaments and the men's World Championship Tennis maintained their popularity, World Team Tennis did not.

Billie Jean King was clearly the independent woman. Her image was reminiscent of the career women films of the 1940s. She appeared at a time when women's issues were being publicly debated and when women discussed having a career and marriage. King combined the two and appeared as a successful social type: a married woman athlete. She lived a new kind of life, one unknown to most women, but one now available and possible to many more. The next generation of women tennis pros, such as Chris Evert Lloyd and Martina Navratilova, had an easier time being accepted as serious and dedicated professionals, thanks to King's pathbreaking actions.

One result of the women's movement was passage of the 1972 Education Amendments; among its goals was the elimination of discrimination in college athletic programs for women. Many colleges began recruiting women athletes in greater numbers than ever before. For example, UCLA tripled its women's inter-collegiate athletic budget in one year.[21] Team sports for women benefited from this action as well.

Nancy Lieberman, a native of New York City born in 1958, was one of the most highly publicized beneficiaries of the new recruiting. Nearly 100 colleges and universities sought her out as she had been an extraordinarily able high school basketball player. She chose Old Dominion College over the larger schools and led their basketball team to an Association for Intercollegiate Athletics for Women (AIAW) championship in 1979. Earlier, in 1976, she had won a silver medal in the Olympics and would have been a member of the 1980 U.S. women's basketball team, if the United States had not boycotted the Moscow games. When she became a professional basketball player in 1981, she was the highest paid woman in the game, reportedly receiving $100,000 a year. There were eight teams in the professional Women's Basketball League (WBL) with Lieberman playing for the Dallas Diamonds. In the previous year, the team had had a 7–28 record, but with her spectacular playing, the Diamonds ended the year with a 32–11 record. Attendance at the games tripled. But, as one reporter noted, "even Lieberman's efforts couldn't solve the league's financial problems, and in November, the WBL collapsed."[22]

During Lieberman's brief tenure with the ill-fated Women's Basketball League, her reputation as an inimitable athlete spread; her fans wore sweatshirts that read, "And on the Eighth Day God Created Nancy Lieberman." The Spalding Sporting Goods Company put her on their advisory staff and maufactured an autographed basketball for her, the first time a woman had been so honored.[23] But Lieberman could not create enough interest in professional women's basketball to sustain the league. In 1982 she and promoter Larry King tried to get corporate sponsorship for a league of four teams, but the financial support was not forthcoming.

Lieberman's unquestioned skill in a male-identified sport made her a popular athlete, but one difficult to define. The journalists, more sensitive in the late 1970s and 1980s to the charge of sexism, did not label her as mannish, as they had done to Babe Didrikson Zaharias in the 1930s, but they found no handy alternative image either. She was surely an independent woman, a pioneer in territory uncharted by women athletes, but was she simply an isolated phenomenon or the beginning of a wave of women basketball players? The failure of the WBL suggested that she was an atypical woman athlete, not a forerunner of a new group.

Lieberman once said about her own relation to the game: "Basketball has opened up a lot of doors for me. But it is a sport—it's not my whole life."[24] Nevertheless, she has tried to create opportunities for other women interested in pursuing a professional career in basketball, but to no avail. The public, though avid spectators of men's basketball, has not shown a similar interest in professional women's basketball. So while tennis players enjoy great public support, the same cannot be said for women basketball players.

As already seen, the small strides women athletes have made has been largely in individual sports, not team athletics. Skating, after tennis and golf, has attracted notice over the years and, especially in an earlier period, was the favored sport for many woman athletes. Perhaps the earliest, outstanding example of a woman skater was Sonja Henie, the Norwegian woman who became a star, not only on ice, but in Hollywood, a true example of the union between sport celebrity and show business fame. Born in Oslo, Norway, in 1913, Henie distinguished herself as a young girl and at 15 won the first of three Olympic medals. For ten consecutive years, she won the World Championship Figure Skating Contest. After this impressive display, she became a professional in 1936 and declared that she also wanted to be a movie star.[25]

Signed by Twentieth Century Fox in 1936 to a five-year contract and two pictures a year, Henie demonstrated her impressive skating skills on the silver screen, thereby increasing her admiring audience by millions. *One in a Million*, released on New Year's Day, 1937, earned an ecstatic review from the *New York Times* film critic Bosley Crowther. Though he acknowledged that the movie's story was a "disconnected variety show,"[26] Sonja Henie's skating enchanted him. Crowther thought that the great movie stars Marlene Dietrich and Greta Garbo looked like earthbound creatures next to the ethereal Henie. Her second movie, *Second Fiddle*, was equally popular with the critics and the audiences. By 1939 the *Motion Picture Herald*'s exhibitors' poll rated her third in box office appeal, just behind child star Shirley Temple and Clark Gable.[27]

Henie organized her own ice show revue, which toured the country yearly. While all the shows were not of equal quality, all commentators noted the extraordinary showmanship of Henie. Her dramatic skating held her audiences entranced, while her ensemble of skaters wore dazzling costumes and skated in front of sets that befitted a Hollywood extravaganza. Henie had capitalized on her skating skills to catapult herself into a highly successful entertainer and entrepreneur. She alienated some people with her expectations for remuneration for everything she did, but she considered it proper. Blonde, slender, and demure looking, she projected an image of sweetness and Mary-like innocence, though her detractors viewed her as mercenary. Her fans accepted Henie's version of herself and flocked to her revues and movies.

Sonja Henie united athletic talent with show business skills; she became a popular cultural star because her skating fascinated her audience and because her skill could be displayed attractively within the format of the movies. She gave up her amateur status as soon as it had accomplished what she sought: public recognition. She was a contemporary of Babe Didrickson and shared with her an unshakable self-confidence, a trait not usually associated with women. Amateurism is considered genteel, a proper female status, not professionalism. But Sonja Henie, Billie Jean King, and the Babe rejected this age-old category and created their own. In so doing, they became highly successful, but atypical women athletes.

Dorothy Hamill (b. 1957) was a skating champion who had a career path with interesting similarities and differences to Sonja Henie. She grew up in Riverside, Connecticut, and began skating when she was eight years old.[28] While Henie hated to practice, and rarely skated more than three hours a day, Hamill skated seven hours a day, every day, to perfect this difficult art. At 17, she won the U.S. Figure Skating Championship, the title that ensured her position as the U.S. representative in the world championships in Munich, Germany, in March 1974.

Hamill was a pretty, petite, young woman who quickly became a favorite with the media and with young women all over the United States. In 1976 she won a gold medal at the Winter Olympics in Innsbruck and returned to the United States as a certified heroine. Young girls began cutting their hair to imitate the Hamill style, while a Hollywood agent was hired to arrange the many offers for endorsements, including ones with Clairol shampoo and a doll company planning to market a Dorothy Hamill doll. She signed on with the Ice Capades and everyone, including her parents, seemed intent on benefiting from her new fame.[29] She was the child-woman, the ingenue Mary who endeared herself to a youth-loving public.

The rapid transformation of an amateur, young skater into a professional celebrity seemed, according to one contemporary observer, to bewilder Hamill. A naturally shy woman, with little worldy experience, she suddenly found herself surrounded by public relations people, the press, and pro-moters of various products. Further, the trials of traveling with the Ice Capades prevented her from making friends or living any kind of normal life.[30] Surely the career of Dorothy Hamill illustrated a modern irony: while women athletes fought for years to achieve recognition, sometimes the few who caught the media's eye have been pushed into superstardom without understanding what happened. Further, their skill, their athletic talent, the basis for their original celebrity status, became less and less significant as their face adorned a wide variety of products in the marketplace. Sonja Henie, Babe Didrikson, and Billie Jean King all achieved fame as adult women who participated in the decision-making process regarding the products they endorsed, the enterprises they engaged in, and the direction their careers took. When a child star such as Dorothy Hamill was elevated to stardom before the accompanying maturity occurred, others determined her career choices, not always to her benefit.

Sports writers unconsciously described women athletes in much the same way that they depicted women entertainers. They tried to fit them into the triad of images. While most were clearly independent women, they ran the risk of being labeled masculine, if their independence was too much in evidence. The very young women athletes, of course, were usually char-acterized as the Marys (Hamill and tennis player Chris Evert Lloyd at the beginning of her career), in contrast to the spunky independent woman (Billie Jean King) or the occasional Eve (tennis player Gussie Moran in the 1940s and contemporary golfer Jan Stephenson).

Audiences and writers seemed most comfortable with the feminine ath-letes, the women who walked the tightrope between being too serious (that is, too competitive) and too flighty (that is, too feminine). While male athletes could exhibit a wide range of traits, from the bawdy to the conventional, women athletes were expected to remain Mary-like, while exhibiting only a genteel amount of independence. Neither their sweat nor their determination was to detract from their attractiveness. Sports remain associated with brutishness, male camaraderie, bald competition, and bravado. Of all the areas of popular culture, it is probably in sports that women have had, and continue to have, the hardest time breaking down stereotypical images and expectations.

A few years ago, the National Gallery in Washington mounted a touring exhibit of photographs of outstanding U.S. athletes. Of 100 athletes so designated, only 9 were women: one swimmer, two golfers, three skaters, two tennis players, and one track star. This representation, statistically 9 percent, is probably an accurate reflection of women's presence in sports. All of the representatives competed in individual sports; most distinguished themselves as amateurs, and, with the exception of Billie Jean King, none would be familiar to contemporary audiences. While popular culture in this country contains many male sports figures in its pantheon of greats, women athletes have not yet achieved such exalted status.

NOTES

1. Summaries of this subject are contained in Robert J. Higgs, "Sports, Race, and Sex," in *Sports, a Reference Guide* (Westport, Conn.: Greenwood Press, 1982), pp. 126–36; Ronald A. Smith, "The Rise of Basketball for Women in Colleges," in Steven A. Riess, ed., *The American Sporting Experience* (West Point, N.Y.: Leisure Press, 1984), pp. 239–54; and Dudley A. Sargent, "Are Athletes Making Girls Masculine?" in Riess, pp. 255–63.

2. Smith, "Basketball for Women," p. 243.

3. Ibid.

4. As late as 1931, according to physical educator Mabel Lee in her survey of 100 colleges, 12 percent allowed intercollegiate athletics. Smith, "Basketball for Women," p. 244.

5. Oliver Jensen, *A College Album* (New York: American Heritage, 1974), p. 37.

6. Higgs, in "Sports, Race, and Sex," p. 129, quotes Clayton L. Thomas who provided evidence of women's physiological ability to compete.

7. Allen Guttmann, *From Ritual to Record: The Nature of Modern Sports* (New York: Columbia University Press, 1978), p. 34.

8. William Oscar Johnson and Nancy P. Williamson, '*Whatta-Gal*': *The Babe Didrikson Story* (Boston: Little Brown, 1977), p. 100.

9. Ibid., p. 142.

10. *Current Biography, 1947,* (New York: H. W. Wilson Co., 1947), p. 702.

11. Ibid., p. 703.

12. Robert Scharff et al., *Golf magazine's Encyclopedia of Golf* (New York: Harper & Row, 1970), pp. 24–25.

13. *Current Biography, 1947,* p. 703.

14. Bud Collins, "Introduction," *Bud Collins' Modern Encyclopedia of Tennis*, eds. Bud Collins and Zander Hollander (Garden City, N.Y.: Doubleday, 1980), p. xix.

15. Stan Isaacs, "Was It Really Golden?" in ibid., p. 32.

16. Billie Jean King with Frank Deford, *Billie Jean* (New York: Viking Press, 1982), p. 13.

17. *Current Viewpoints*, November 1974, p. 13.

18. Curry Kirkpatrick, "There She Is, Ms America," *Sports Illustrated*, October 1, 1973, p. 32.

19. The other televised tennis match that expanded the popularity of tennis, according to Collins, was the 1972 World Championship Tennis match between Rod Laver and Ken Rosewall. See Collins, *Encyclopedia of Tennis*, p. xix.

20. Billie Jean King with Kim Chapin, *Billie Jean* (New York: Harper & Row, 1974), p. 142. Also consult the 1982 autobiography for a discussion of this topic.

21. Cheryl M. Fields, "Big Gains for Women's Sports," *Chronicle of Higher Education*, December 9, 1974, p. 7.

22. "A Basketball Star Tries a New Angle," *Newsweek*, March 22, 1982, p. 16.

23. Ibid. and Steve Wulf, "A Girl Who's Just One of the Guys," *Sports Illustrated*, July 21, 1980, p. 20.

24. Basketball Star Tries a New Angle," p. 16E.

25. Information on Sonja Henie can be found in *Current Biography, 1940*, (New York: H. W. Wilson Co., 1940) pp. 380–82, and "Ice Queen," *Time*, February 2, 1948, pp. 50–54.

26. Bosley Crowther, "One in a Million," *New York Times*, January 1, 1937, p. 19.

27. *Current Biography, 1940*, (New York: H. W. Wilson Co., 1940) p. 381.

28. J. Bruce, "Divine Right of Queens," *Sports Illustrated*, February 18, 1974, pp. 66+ and Philip Taubman, "The Exploitation of Dorothy Hamill," *Esquire*, May 23, 1978, pp. 34–40.

29. Taubman, "Dorothy Hamill," p. 36.

30. Ibid.

10

Women Stars of the 1980s

Living in the late twentieth century in the United States gives most people longer, healthier lives. This phenomenon has interesting, and important, ramifications for women entertainers: more generations of popular women stars continue to live and work in the 1980s. Lucille Ball still appears, in new series after new series, on prime time television. Jane Wyman, the 1940s movie star, is the matriarch on the nightime melodrama "Falcon Crest," and singer Dinah Shore is still doing live concerts. They all coexist in the diverse popular cultural market; women in their forties such as Jane Fonda, Barbra Streisand, Bette Midler, and Liza Minelli, stars in their fifties like Shirley MacLaine, Anne Bancroft, and Bea Arthur, as well as younger women like Whitney Houston, Madonna, Ally Sheedy, and Molly Ringwald all find multigenerational audiences, though the younger stars appeal primarily to their own age group.

All of the popular women stars project the same dominant images of earlier generations, though with interesting variations. Older women can be strong matriarchal types, independent women, with impunity, while younger women in charge are still viewed with suspicion. The middle generation of women can play any of the three traditional roles; they may appear as vulnerable victims, mature seductresses, or career women, or a combination of all three images. Young women can be sweet Marys, tempting Eves, and feisty independents. There is more blending of images currently than ever before. In this sense, rich and diverse syntheses offer audiences interesting alterations on well-worn and well-liked themes.

Sometimes, the stars are able to transform their image over time to accommodate changing circumstances. Sweet Mary Tyler Moore became known as a serious actress; her film portrayal of an unfeeling mother in *Ordinary People* and her theatrical performance in *Whose Life Is It Anyway?* (both in 1980) established her as a serious actress with depth and breadth. Similarly, comic Carol Burnett has successfully acted in movies and television dramas. In other instances, it is the times that change and rediscover the actress who typified an earlier, cherished image; the constant reappearance of Dinah Shore in one popular cultural medium or another is a good example of this phenomenon. With people in the United States living longer lives, popular cultural producers have to include older people in their television series and their movies. So Anne Baxter (on "Hotel" until her death), Barbara Stanwyck (on "The Colbys), Jane Wyman (on "Falcon Crest"), and Barbara Bel Geddes (on "Dallas") all portrayed matriarchs, a realistic, but newer, image in an aging nation.

Not only do at least three generations of popular women performers coexist, but they also cross over into each other's territory. Singer Whitney Houston is planning to make a movie, while Madonna has made two, and movie stars such as Jessica Lange and Sissy Spacek played singers in movies about real-life women, Patsy Kline and Loretta Lynn respectively. Further, musical stars often appeared on television, either in specials or on the new phenomenon of the 1980s: music television. Madonna, indeed, became a star thanks to MTV. In this new medium, the singer acted out the lyrics of her song in a dramatically rendered production, thereby creating a minidrama, a context for the song. The singer got the opportunity to display whatever acting ability she had as well. These music videos could also be purchased separately. Thus, music, television, and the movies intermingled, with the stars performing on every one of the dominant media.

Pop music and television seemed healthier than the movies for women entertainers. Though the stars still wanted to make movies, there were fewer opportunities; according to a recent study, teenagers, the primary moviegoers, reduced their attendance of movies by 20 percent in 1985, while tripling their rental of video films.[1] The public remained ardent consumers of mass entertainment, but the dominant role of the movies has been seriously diminished. Further, the young male moviegoers, 14 to 24 years old, say the market researchers, only go to watch male heroes on screen. The family audience of the movies in the 1930s and 1940s is no more. At best, women movie stars can hope to make one movie every two or three years, in stark contrast to three movies a year by Bette Davis.

Yet, as critic David Thomson has suggested, women performers continue to want to make movies; in his opinion, television has treated women better:

"The snobbery persists that TV work is hurried, down-scale, and inferior. Movies are where serious actresses or ambitious showbiz personalities should go."[2] Thomson pointed to the careers of Goldie Hawn (who has not equaled her fame on Rowan and Martin's "Laugh-In"), Tyne Daley (whose screen career never matched her success on "Cagney and Lacey"), Shelley Long (whose work on "Cheers" made the show popular), and Ann-Margret (whose most serious performances have been in TV films rather than theatrical features where she played a sex-pot).[3] Despite this interesting view, and despite the fact that movies continued to be made in record quantities, women sought screen roles but did not find them.

When women appeared in each and every medium, their images remained largely within the three dominant ones analyzed throughout this book. That is no surprise or mystery: they describe primal characteristics of women. It was the either/or quality and its simplistic expression that has received criticism by some commentators. When popular culture makers presented interesting, exciting, and unusual blends of the images, they were greeted with approval. When they recognized that the types were not mutually exclusive but rather interactive, and present in all women, they created authentic heroines for the audiences to admire. This subject will be covered in greater detail at the end of the chapter.

The new generation of popular cultural stars operates within a preexisting tradition. They do not appear in a vacuum, nor do they act outside of history. Most study their predecessors, learn the customs of their field, the routes to success, and the reasons for failure. For many, the past may only be the previous five years; nevertheless, they consciously demonstrate their awareness of the fact that they are entering a field with a history and a set of traditions. They try to build on or depart from that past. If they appear as merely a clone to a previously successful star, they usually fail. Though imitation is a form of admiration, novelty, which is ardently sought in the popular cultural world, requires constant change or at least the semblance of change. But even the change appears as a reaction to, or a variation of, a previous style.

Whitney Houston (b. 1963), a young black singer who has made a quick rise to the top of the popular musical charts, is a good example of a woman who acknowledges the rich cultural roots and family environment that nourished her singing. Raised in a musical home (her mother Cissy Houston is an experienced pop and gospel singer), she began singing in church as a young woman in East Orange, New Jersey.[4] Her first cousin is the well-regarded veteran singer Dionne Warwick. Singing spiritual and gospel music prior to popular music also places Houston within a long line of successful black and white women singers who followed that course. The church singing of Dolly Parton gave her the experience and background that became useful to her in the popular musical field as well.

The one factor that distinguishes the young singer who comes out of a religious tradition today is that she thinks nothing of crossing over into the secular pop field, whereas the great gospel singer Mahalia Jackson would never consider singing earthly songs. Also, thanks to professional management and skilled producers, talented singers receive a lot of publicity quickly and achieve celebrity status within a short period of time. Houston's debut album of 1986 sold 7 million copies by the end of the year.[5] Three of the hit singles from the album displayed her subject matter: "Saving All My Love For You," "How Will I Know?" and "The Greatest Love of All." Houston's big voice and powerful delivery were used to sing traditional romantic lyrics in a bombastic, soft rock format. While her style placed her within the modern pop music category, her words connected her with blues and pop singers of the past.

Singer Madonna borrowed from the older bawdy women tradition and the newer rock and roll subculture. She appeared on stage as the daring, shocking woman. Her fans flocked to her concerts at Madison Square Garden to watch their heroine act out in person her "Material Girl" song as well as "Like a Virgin." Her more recent bestseller, "Poppa Don't Preach" describes a pregnant young unmarried woman's plea to her father that he should give support in her wish to keep the child and begin a new life with the man she loves.

A reporter's description of a 1985 Madonna concert in Los Angeles demonstrates how Madonna, a product of the 1980s, combined bawdiness, rock, and the ambivalence toward growing up that seem to characterize youth of the time. The reviewer told how she continually asked her audience if they were excited and responded to their screechings by writhing across the stage in her peacock paisley top, denim micro-mini, and blue suede ankle boots. She danced and moved around constantly; knowingly or unknowingly, Madonna behaved on the stage very much like Eva Tanguay did 70 years earlier. Yet, concluded the reviewer, "Somehow, despite the hard core moves, Madonna did not really come off as naughty or menacing so much as solicitous and good hearted, a kind of flirtatious, sugary sex fairy whose outrageous poses were really just a gift to the kids, a fantasy offering to help them grow up."[6]

The imagery contained in this illustration suggests a Mary/Eve combination, a young woman who gives off strong sexual feelings while remaining sweet and pure. Surely the prepubescent girls who comprised a large part of her audience were not ready for the mature sexual message of Madonna. The exaggerated outfits, the theatrical performance, and the suggestive, if not explicit, lyrics distinguished her from her competitors. No commentator raves about her voice; indeed, many mentioned its thinness and nasal quality. But it was her performance, her persona, as the good-bad girl that attracted the audience and her particular way of demonstrating that combination of images. The young women of the 1980s seized both images simultaneously, and Madonna personified it for them.

Another unlikely contributor to the Mary/Eve blend was Pat Benatar, sometimes called the Queen of Hard Rock. Her reputation was established as one of the very few women who could outshout the men singers and screech out angry lyrics that dared men to betray her. Recently, she softened her image and though she still sang "Love Is a Battlefield" and "Hit Me With Your Best Shot," she introduced sweeter songs such as "Run Between the Raindrops" and her hit "(Stop Using) Sex As a Weapon," in which she called for the end of the power struggle between the sexes. Her audiences knew of her personal disappointments in the arena of love and that she had recently given birth to a child, an experience that moderated her previously harsh view of life.[7] Because the fans perceived her concerts as a form of interaction between the star and themselves, they empathized with her troubles and her changes.

Women singers shared, with some of their predecessors, a consuming interest in the subject of sex. Perhaps because they sang mainly romantic songs, the subject of love, and its modern equivalent, sex, occupied their thoughts and their lyrics. It is in their discussion of women's sexuality that they expressed their differences from their ancestors. It is also in the greater liberality of the times that their words are tolerated. Bessie Smith sang of love lost and love sought, and Sophie Tucker made fun of many of the unspoken myths about women's feelings toward sex. Eva Tanguay and Mae West played many of the same themes as Madonna and Cyndi Lauper, but the one dramatic difference is that contemporary performers can sing publicly in a large concert hall lyrics that sent Mae West to jail and threatened to do the same to Sophie Tucker. In the relatively limited confines of a burlesque house, to a male-only audience, Tucker and West could get away with their risqué stories, songs, and gestures, but not in the family-oriented vaudeville palaces.

One of the continuous images has been that of the bawdy woman entertainer, the naughtiest of Eves. Mae West, her imitators and followers, appeared time and again. Ethel Merman, on the 1940s Broadway stage, was regularly compared to her while Tina Turner is called the Mae West of Rock. In the 1970s, Bette Midler parodied Sophie Tucker routines. While Eva Tanguay probably inspired both West and Tucker, she is unknown to contemporary audiences though her persona lives on through the others. The power of bawdiness persists alongside the other basic qualities satisfied by the three images.

One student of the lyrics of popular music in recent decades, unaware of the bawdy women singers, claimed that in the 1980s for the first time women sang songs in which they initiated the sexual encounter with men; in earlier decades, she argued, they were notably passive, waiting for the man they loved to take action. One recent example offered was the song "Magic" by Olivia Newton-John in which she took the dominant role, led the man, and caught him when he fell. Perhaps a more accurate comment would be that these bold sentiments never had the popular airing they do today, thanks to a more permissive public and to an affluent youth group who buys records without parental knowledge or approval, features of life in recent years only.

All three young singers, Houston, Madonna, and Benatar, aptly displayed the transitional and uncertain qualities of 1980s popular culture. Their embrace of inconsistent, if not contradictory, images demonstrated that nothing and everything is "in" simultaneously. Another plausible explanation is that they believe that all three images coexist harmoniously in each woman. She can be Eve/Mary/independent woman simultaneously. So young actresses attempt to carve out atypical, unstereotypic portrayals while playing traditional images. Thanks to the women's liberation movement of the last decade, actresses and entertainers discuss their feelings about the roles they choose publicly; they display far more independence in selecting roles than ever before. Actress Jane Fonda, who had been identified with feminist-heroine roles in movies of the 1970s, recently played an alcoholic, down-and-out actress in a 1986 movie *The Morning After*. She said of her choice: "I was getting a little angry at the idea that all of my roles had to be role models or uplifting examples of exemplary behavior. I'm an actress. I like to play all kinds of women."[8]

Personal taste, rather than philosophical position or stereotypical typecasting, seems to be the criterion for choosing roles, at least for independent-minded, and perhaps financially independent, stars. The lessons derived from the women's movement vary from interpreter to interpreter. Fonda no longer cares to play role models exclusively; other feminists have suggested that all stereotypes are to be rejected; and film critic Molly Haskell has claimed that the residue left by the 1970s women's liberation movement was a desire by the audience to see strong women in film, but the *way* that the women showed their strength was irrelevant.[9] At the same time, however, the male establishment of Hollywood feared strong women and thus still avoided the subject, according to Haskell, by ignoring women and making mainly nymphet movies or thrillers where women were superfluous. Alternatively, sensitive social dramas were produced in which men dealt with problems usually associated with women. For example, in *Kramer vs. Kramer*, Dustin Hoffman had to cope with a career and raising a child. Sex role reversal, in this case, was utilized to avoid featuring women. Haskell continues: "There are more of us who want to 'do it all' or 'have it all', and more areas in which to feel anxious and inadequate."[10] She also has claimed that women themselves are not sure how they should be portrayed: as victims or heroines.

Victims, of course, have always been contained within the Mary image, while the heroine was a form of independent woman or a successful Eve. But there are great differences between the victim/heroine, and the triad of images described in this book. The former perspective shows a recent feminist awareness of women's treatment, while the latter suggests cultural symbols that have had a long life in Western history. The triad, in my view, is a richer and more accurate summary of women's depictions, rather than the reductive, simplistic dualism. The melding of images often made for a very human and sympathetic portrayal of women. Both sexes are assertive and passive, dependent and independent, each at different times and circumstances. Women are not always victims or heroines. Sometimes, they are neither—or both.

Surely it is gratifying to avoid one-dimensional portraits of women; that is important for moral, esthetic, and entertainment purposes. When Hollywood or television does that, audiences displayed their appreciation by watching the movie or television show. *Aliens*, a science fiction adventure of 1986, offered a good example of a reworked stereotype that is attractive and very popular. The movie also provided evidence of the evolution of tastes and values in the United States. The great reception received by *Aliens* suggested that feminist values have had a positive effect on the public. Outer space adventures have had a long history in U.S. popular culture. But the central character was always male, and the woman, if she were present, played a secondary role.

In *Aliens* Sigourney Weaver, a new actress of the 1980s, played the heroic role; she was the only survivor of a previous exploration to an outer colony and reluctantly returned, with a new crew, to find and destroy the enemy. What transpired in this conventional formula film was a very humane treatment of a thrilling, dangerous subject. Weaver combined the warmth and concern associated with women and the skill and leadership qualities associated with men. She comforted and protected the child-survivor, took charge when the male expedition leader and his second in command failed, and destroyed the enemy.

Weaver's character was a successful example of sex role reversal; she was a woman performing a traditionally male role, and she did it ably. The box office success of the movie proved that audiences accepted women as space leaders. The formula of the thriller continued to appeal to many, and its success suggested that all formulas could be recast with women in the central roles. Imagine women as the adventurers while men became the objects of domestic comedies; both sexes could be lovers, and both could be hurt and helped in melodramas. Though the fundamental images and conventions endure, in the transitional 1980s, both sexes could play a wider range of images, a greater variety of human possibilities.

Television series also seem to be in a state of flux. Whereas television seasons used to last the school year (from September to June), shows are now terminated after 6, 8, or 12 weeks. New series join the program schedule in every month of the season. In the early history of television, studios allowed time, sometimes a season or two, for a show to find its audience; today, the Nielsen ratings judge a show each week, and the network chiefs cancel shows within months of their debut. This situation made it difficult for new, experimental shows to develop new concepts, new images, and new ideas. "Cagney and Lacey," for example, began slowly, was cancelled due to low ratings, and only returned to prime time television after a concerted letter-writing campaign to the network by its small, but loyal, following. Its history, however, is unusual. A canceled show is usually lost and forgotten very quickly.

According to a recent study, of the 68 series on television in the 1986–87 year, only three focused upon the traditional family. The situation comedy, which always featured women, albeit sweet Marys, has returned in great number to late 1980s television; but the makeup of the family has changed radically from the 1950s and 1960s versions. No longer is mom, dad, and the kids the dominant model, nor is the newsroom the surrogate family; rather grandmothers, grandfathers, boarders, strangers, and assorted others now participate in family life. Servants dictate to family members, and children are often the smartest people of all.[11] Women do not fare particularly well in this new, unusual setting. Indeed, as this study noted, while single-family households have increased in real life, and are primarily headed by women, on television, of the six situation comedies with single parents, five were headed by men.[12]

In the 1970s, perhaps the Golden Era for women in television, there were Maud, Lucy, Mary, Alice, Phyllis, Laverne, and Shirley. They were among the many women stars in situation comedies. Though many began as conventional comedic types, they evolved into more complex personalities. Alice was both humorous and independent, never the nitwit. The mother in "One Day at a Time," a divorcee raising two children alone, experienced both humorous and bittersweet moments. Similarly, Laverne and Shirley were working women, and Mary was a career woman looking for romance. All of these women stretched the boundaries of the traditional situation comedy. Their material was a major departure from "Ozzie and Harriet" and the "Dick Van Dyke Show." They were modern women coping, often humorously, with the difficulties and frustrations of daily life.

In the 1980s situation comedies, there are fewer women and less diversity in their characterizations. Though the mothers on both "Family Ties" and "The Cosby Show" are professional women, they are rarely portrayed working. It is their mother role that is featured; they are shown at home, not in the office. A recent study by the National Commission on Working Women found that working-class women are underrepresented on television, while professional women are overrepresented. Also, while Hispanic and Asian women are increasing their numbers in real life, they are virtually nonexistent on television shows. Black women, though often acting in the roles of maids, a traditional stereotype, are numerically overrepresented according to the study.[13]

One of the tentative trends of the late 1980s seems to be the acknowl-edgement of the independent woman as an authentic type, but it is a soft-ened, blurred portrait rather than the sharply defined one in the movies of the 1930s and 1940s. The independent woman on 1980s television might be a doctor or an architect, but she is a mother, a wife, and a family member. In the words of today, she has her priorities in order and does not let her career dominate her life. The Sigourney Weaver character in *Aliens* took time to comfort the child before pursuing the enemy. Phylicia Rashad, the wife-mother-lawyer on "The Cosby Show" is always available for her children.

There is a mixed message in this new depiction of independent women. Though working, they describe the fantasy element far more than reality. Most women working do not have glamorous jobs, nor do they "have it all." It is also ironic that, now that women work in large numbers, work is devalued for them while it has always been the most important single ingredient in the man's self-definition. Work is subsumed in popular culture for women while the traditional definition of her as wife and mother is reasserted. In "Kate and Allie," one of the best situation comedies featuring women, two divorced women, one with two children and the other with one, share a New York City townhouse. Kate, played by Susan St. James, is a travel agent while Allie, played by Jane Curtin, stays home, cooks, and acts as the traditional homemaker. The primary thrust of the comedy comes from the children's school and social problems. Thus, as well written and acted as this series is, it still remains within the standard situation comedy format.

Television acknowledged the 1980s by portraying divorced mothers, dis-cussions of sexuality, drugs, and crime, and featuring extended families, but the basic value system with the woman staying at home persisted. So women may have become independent, but it is a reluctantly acquired independence, born of necessity and not desire.

There seem to be varying paths for enduring women stars: they may become superstars with multigenerations of fans by doing one thing better than anyone else: the comic antics of Lucy, the heroics of Hepburn, Dinah Shore as Dinah Shore, the blues of Bessie Smith, or the role of Mary Richards by Mary Tyler Moore. Scintillating Eves such as Elizabeth Taylor continue to enjoy popularity; her face appears on magazine covers in the 1980s almost as frequently as it did in the 1950s. Currently, her personal life offers the dramatic subject matter that used to characterize her film portrayals.

A rarer form of durability is when the entertainer does many things very well: Barbra Streisand as a singer of various styles of song, as a comic, a serious actress, and a movie director and producer. A third possibility, achieved through both skill and good timing, is when a star moves from one successful vehicle to another. Bea Arthur played the popular loudmouth Maud on 1970s television and in the mid–1980s returned to television sit-coms with "The Golden Girls," a show about three older women. Mary Tyler Moore appeared in a hit show on Broadway in early 1987.

Two stars who have demonstrated their longevity are Barbra Streisand and Bette Midler. Streisand (b. 1942) has been discussed in this book in terms of her film career, while her singing has been briefly mentioned. During the 1980s, her career appeared to be in the decline. Hollywood failed to reward her production of *Yentl* (1983), and her 1985 record album *Emotion* was her lowest charting album in 15 years. In late 1985, however, against all advice, she recorded Broadway hits, primarily by composer Stephen Sondheim. Within two months of the album's release, *The Broadway Album* sold 2 million copies.[14] Streisand still had the formula for success. In De-cember 1986 she appeared in her first full-length television concert in 20 years. "Barbra Streisand: One Voice" had been taped earlier in the year by cable television's Home Box Office at her home in Malibu. Streisand staged the event as a fundraiser for the Hollywood Women's Political Committee. She raised the largest sum to date for a one-night live performance in California.[15] Recent reports suggest that she is working on another movie as well as a movie musical.

Bette Midler, (b. 1945), whom movie critic Molly Haskell called "the strongest woman to hit the stage or screen since Mae West,"[16] has also seen failures along with successes in recent years. Her 1981 movie *Jinxed* was a box office failure, and commentators wondered whether the Midler magic had dimmed. But in 1986 she appeared in two hit comedies, *Down and Out in Beverly Hills* and *Ruthless People*. In both, Midler showed her irrepressible wit, her anarchic tendencies, and her willingness to make fun of everyone, including herself. Midler had a baby in 1986 and appeared in a third hit comedy, *Outrageous Fortune*. She shows no signs of slowing down.

The collective power of Streisand and Midler may be based upon their ability to project the trio of women's images. Though neither woman is beautiful by conventional standards, they are both still physically appealing; their highly sympathetic personas allow audiences to identify with them and visualize them in various settings, including romantic ones. Indeed, they may be representative of the coda of the late 1980s: Eves/Marys/ independent women who defy the expected portraits. Neither of these two women, nor movie stars Streep and Field, nor singers Madonna and Cyndi Lauper, are conventionally beautiful. In the late 1980s, heroines can be romantic without being tragically lovely à la Greta Garbo or Elizabeth Taylor. They can be seductive without looking temptuous. And they can combine their Eve qualities with sweetness and vulnerability.

Critics described both Whitney Houston and Madonna as innocent and seductive simultaneously, traits that are seemingly contradictory. The stars of the 1980s want to have it all and so do their audiences; so they project images that contain aspects of the three-sided nature of woman. They embrace all three images and ignore the contradictions, or perhaps acknowledge human inconsistency as a given. Meryl Streep projects strength and weakness as do Midler and Streisand; they have extended the stereotypes by combining them. Unwittingly perhaps, in their search for unstereotypic portraits, they have reshaped the archetypal images.

This point captures a paradox characteristic of many of the new feminist stars of the 1980s. They interpret the message of feminism to mean: be your own unique person. Accordingly, they attempt to distinguish themselves from all others, to mark themselves off as unusual, different, even bizarre. Surely the rock subculture, out of which many of the current women singers emerge, also contributed to the sometimes grotesque extremes to which they went. Madonna's belly button, her audacious lyrics, and her willingness to be the bad girl publicly is a combination of rock's endless search for the weird, and the franker atmosphere resulting from liberation rhetoric in the 1970s.

While feminism surely heralded the right of women to express themselves, it acknowledged the legitimacy of all dimensions of their nature: their Mary/Eve/independent qualities. Feminism proclaimed the right of women to be any or all of these things simultaneously. It rejected rigid classifications for women and men; and it denied absolute categories of being that extinguished or diminished human possibility. Intelligent, respectful portrayals of women as wives, mothers, careerists, volunteers, and sexual beings were all welcomed from a feminist perspective.

Feminist actresses Jessica Lange and Meryl Streep often sought film scripts that broke all of the stereotypes. They wanted each script to depart from all established patterns and, thus, sought to escape the archetypal features of the triad of images described in these pages. However, there are real problems with this view. It is hard to imagine female characters that do not possess at least some aspect of the trio. These human features of woman cannot be overcome because they are integral to her being. Pragmatically, by building a film career on unique, unrepeatable personas, the actress fails to create the loyalty of the audience. Of the actresses who emerged in the 1970s, Sally Field remains one of the few who has portrayed a consistent type, that of the spunky independent. From *Norma Rae* to *Places in the Heart*, she portrayed film characters who came from modest family backgrounds and, through courage and self-determination, survived. Audiences, then, came to expect her to be the working class independent woman who not only endured hardship, but overcame it.

By contrast, another newcomer to film, Kathleen Turner, looks different in each of her screen portrayals and plays such a range of types that it is hard to build audience support: from the Eve in *Body Heat* to the lighthearted heroine in *Romancing the Stone* and *The Jewel of the Nile*, to the efficient hired killer in the spoof *Prizzi's Honor*, to the soon-to-be divorced homemaker in *Peggy Sue Got Married*. Her very versatility could also be seen as a liability in this context. It prevented her from creating, and remaining true to, a specific image that she could explore over time. Of course, opportunities for provocative roles and the availability of worthy scripts are important considerations that she had little control over.

The close connection between image and star has advantages: it allows fans to identify a desirable set of traits with a favorite star; it enables stars and filmmakers to explore multiple and varied dimensions to the type; and it offers viewers compatible and contrasting visions of the nature of women through their favorite stars. The greatness of Hepburn, for example, was based upon the essential unity of her predictable image and her unique personality. All of the great performers brought something of themselves to the role they played. The harmony of the predictable and predictive role/image with the specialness and difference of the personality of the actress endeared her to her fans. Knowing that Sally Field's character would face adversity, but would surely overcome it, was a major part of the appeal. Kathleen Turner and Meryl Streep's virtuosity made it harder to identify with them. It is also difficult to create unique characters repeatedly.

While contemporary movie stars differ as to how to define themselves, television stars who perform in a weekly series do not have the same problem. They quickly become identified with the character they play in the series. The success of a television series is based upon predictability and continuity from week to week; it does not require, nor does it desire, marked differences in the characters each week. Indeed, many television stars often have problems making the transition to another show or medium. Mary Tyler Moore and Carol Burnett are the exceptions.

In popular culture, the tentative 1980s might be slowly, but surely, moving toward a richer merger of women's images. Independent women may eventually be able to show themselves in all of their diversity. Many interesting melodramas, adventures, and comedies could be created based upon whole independent women. The simple lessons of earlier decades might be replaced with more sophisticated, truer visions. No longer would women be punished for their independence, as they were in the movies of the 1940s, nor would they have to abandon their independence in order to win their man, as they did in the movies of the 1930s. In popular cultural renditions of the 1990s, it might even be possible to see women who are not endlessly preoccupied with finding a man. Romance surely would remain an important subject, but possibly not the most important one.

The images described in this book represent essential features of women and men. We all are, or wish to be, independent, sweet, and sexy. We all wish to be brave, decisive, and faithful. The ideal types always appear as precisely that: ideals to be pursued, though rarely attained. Popular cultural makers implicitly understand the power of the images, and they use that awareness to create likable and sympathetic heroes and heroines. With more consciousness, sensitivity, and respectfulness, they could redefine and re-shape the images in a more humane way; in so doing, they could create enduring values and ideal images of women that would truly be worthy of emulation.

NOTES

1. *Daily Variety*, February 24, 1986, p. 1.

2. David Thomson, "Tuesday's Sisters," *Film Comment*, March–April 1985, p. 33.

3. Ibid.

4. "Whitney Houston: For Talented Young Star, Singing Is A Family Tradition," *Ebony*, December 1985, p. 155.

5. Laura Emerick, "Whitney Houston, Lighten Up," *Chicago Sun-Times*, "Show" section, December 21, 1986, p. 6.

6. Enry, "Madonna Concert Review," *Variety*, May 8, 1985, p. 172.

7. Enry, "Pat Benatar Concert Review," *Variety*, February 5, 1986, p. 15.

8. Roger Ebert, " 'Morning After' Is Murder For Fonda," *Chicago Sun-Times*, "Show" section, December 14, 1986, p. 3.

9. Molly Haskell, "Women in the Movies Grow Up," *Psychology Today*, January 1983, pp. 18–27.

10. Ibid., p. 20.

11. Harry F. Waters, "Overextending the Family," *Newsweek*, November 24, 1986, pp. 76–78.

12. Ibid., p. 77.

13. Susan B. Garland, "TV idealizes the status of Working Women," *Chicago Sun-Times*, "Living" section, December 7, 1986, p. 2. Sixty-one percent of women on the fall season's shows were depicted as professionals, whereas in real life the figure was 23 percent. Black women are 12 percent of the population and 21 percent of the characters on televisions's prime time series in 1986–87.

14. Cathleen McGuigan, "Nice to Have You Back Where You Belong," *Newsweek*, December 23, 1985, p. 77.

15. A. Smith, "Rare indeed," in "TV Prevue" section, *Chicago Sun-Times*, December 21, and 27, 1986, p. 67.

16. Haskell, "Women in the Movies," p. 18.

Selected Bibliography

Of all the popular media discussed in this book, movies have had the most press treatment while popular music has received the least, except for features on pop stars. Women television stars have sometimes been discussed in newspaper articles, but there have been no sustained analyses of television shows or programming for women. Books, newspaper articles, and magazine essays cited in the notes at the end of each chapter are not included in the following bibliography.

NEWSPAPERS, MAGAZINES, AND JOURNALS

Chicago Sun-Times. 1980–86.
Current Biography.
Film Comment. 1984–85.
Film Heritage. Vol. 11, no. 2 (Winter 1975–76).
Film Quarterly. 1982–85.
Films in Review.
Journal of American Culture. 1980–86.
Journal of Broadcasting. 1981–84.
Journal of Broadcasting and Electronic Media. 1985–86.
Journal of Communication. 1985–86.
Journal of Popular Culture. 1980–86.
Journal of Popular Film. 1980–86.

Variety (Daily). 1986
Variety (Weekly). 1984–86.
Velvet Light Trap. Vol. 6 (Fall 1972).

UNPUBLISHED DISSERTATIONS

Dresner, Zita Zatkin, *Twentieth Century American Women Humorists.* College Park: University of Maryland, Ph.D., 1982.

Staples, Shirley Louise, *From "Barney's Courtship" to Burns and Allen: Male-Female Comedy Teams in American Vaudeville, 1865–1932.* Medford, Mass.: Tufts University, Ph.D., 1981.

BOOKS

Adler, Richard P., ed. *Understanding Television: Essays on Television as a Social and Cultural Force.* New York: Praeger, 1981.

Albertsen, Chris. *Bessie.* New York: Stein and Day, 1972.

Atkins, Thomas R. *Sexuality in the Movies.* Bloomington: Indiana University Press, 1975.

Barnouw, Erik. *Tube of Plenty: The Evolution of American Television.* New York: Oxford University Press, 1975.

Baxter, John. *Hollywood in the Thirties.* New York: A. S. Barnes, 1968.

Bergman, Andrew. *We're in the Money: Depression America and Its Films.* New York: Harper Colophon, 1971.

Bonderoff, Jason. *Mary Tyler Moore.* New York: St. Martin's Press, 1986.

Blythe, Cheryl, and Susan Sachett. *Say Goodnight, Gracie!* New York: E. P. Dutton, 1986.

Cantor, Muriel. *Prime-time Television: Content and Control.* Beverly Hills: Sage, 1980.

Daniels, Arlene Kaplan, and James Benet, eds. *Hearth and Home: Images of Women in the Mass Media.* New York: Oxford Univerrsity Press, 1978.

Deming, Barbara. *Running Away From Myself: A Dream Portrait of America Drawn from the Films of the Forties.* New York: Grossman, 1969.

Douglas, George H. *Women of the 20s.* Dallas: Saybrook, 1986.

Erens, Patricia. *Sexual Strategems: The World of Women in Film.* New York: Horizon Press, 1977.

Ewen, David. *Great Men of American Popular Song.* Englewood Cliffs, N.J.: Prentice-Hall, 1970.

Fissinger, Laura. *Tina Turner.* New York: Ballantine Books, 1985.

Gitlin, Todd. *Inside Prime Time.* New York: Pantheon, 1985.

Haskell, Molly. *From Reverence to Rape.* New York: Holt, Rinehart and Winston, 1974.

Intintoli, Michael James. *Taking Soaps Seriously.* New York: Praeger, 1984.

Kael, Pauline. *Kiss, Kiss, Bang Bang.* Boston: Little Brown, 1968.

Kaminsky, Stuart. *American Film Genres.* New York: Dell, 1974.

Kaplan, Janice. *Women and Sports.* New York: Avon Books, 1979.

Kay, Karyn, and Gerald Peary, eds. *Women and the Cinema: A Critical Anthology.* New York: E. P. Dutton, 1977.

Kinkle, Roger D. *The Complete Encyclopedia of Popular Music and Jazz 1900–1950*. Vol. 2. New Rochelle, N.Y.: Arlington House, 1974.

Klinkowitz, Jerome. *The American 1960s: Imaginative Acts In a Decade of Change*. Ames: Iowa State University Press, 1980.

Laufe, Abe. *Broadway's Greatest Musicals*. New York: Funk & Wagnalls, 1977.

Levin, Martin, ed. *Hollywood and the Great Fan Magazine*. New York: Arbor House, 1970.

Lichtenstein, Grace. *A Long Way Baby*. New York: William Morrow, 1974.

Lieb, Sandra R. *Mother of the Blues*. Boston: University of Massachusetts Press, 1981.

McArthur, Benjamin. *Actors and American Culture, 1880–1920. Philadelphia: Temple University Press, 1984.*

McLean, Jr., Albert F. *American Vaudeville as Ritual*. Lexington: University of Kentucky Press, 1965.

Marc, David. *Demographic Vistas: Television in American Culture*. Philadelphia: University of Pennsylvania Press, 1984.

Marion, Frances. *Off With Their Heads*. New York: Macmillan, 1972.

Martin, Linda, and Kerry Segrave. *Women in Comedy*. Secaucus, N.J.: Citadel Press, 1986.

Mellen, Joan. *Women and Their Sexuality in the New Film*. New York: Horizon Press, 1974.

Miller, Randall M., ed. *The Kaleidoscopic Lens: How Hollywood Views Ethnic Groups*. Englewood Cliffs, N.J.: Jerorme S. Ozer, 1980.

Minsky, Morton, and Milt Machlin. *Minsky's Burlesque*. New York: Arbor House, 1986.

Newcomb, Horace. *TV, The Most Popular Art*. New York: Anchor Press, 1974.

Nye, Russell. *The Unembarrassed Muse*. New York: Dial Press, 1970.

Pavletich, Aida. *Rock-A-Bye Baby*. Garden City: Doubleday & Co., 1980.

Remley, Mary L., ed. *Women in Sport: A Guide to Information Sources*. Detroit: Gale Research, 1980.

Ringgold, Gene. *The Films of Bette Davis*. New York: Citadel Press, 1966.

Rosen, Marjorie. *Popcorn Venus*. New York: Coward, McCann, and Geoghagan, 1973.

Schatz, Thomas. *Hollywood Genres: Formulas, Filmmaking, and the Studio System*. Philadelphia: Temple University Press, 1981.

Shaw, Arnold. *The Rock Revolution*. New York: Crowell-Collier Press, 1969.

Slide, Anthony. *Early American Cinema*. New York: A. S. Barnes, 1970.

Stoddard, Karen M. *Saints and Shrews: Women and Aging in American Popular Film*. Westport, Conn.: Greenwood Press, 1983.

Turner, Tina, with Kurt Loder. *I, Tina*. New York: Morrow, 1986.

Wakefield, Dan. *All Her Children*. New York: Doubleday, 1976.

Weibel, Kathryn. *Mirror, Mirror: Images of Women Reflected in Popular Culture*. Garden City, N.Y.: Anchor Press, 1977.

Welsch, Janice R. *Film Archetypes: Sisters, Mistresses, Mothers and Daughters*. New York: Arno Press, 1978.

Window Dressing on the Set: Women and Minorities in Television. A Report of the U.S. Commission on Civil Rights. August, 1977.

ARTICLES

Denisoff, Serge, and John Bridges. "Popular Music: Who Are the Recording Artists?" *Journal of Communication* v. 32 Winter 1982, pp. 132–42.

"Don't Laugh When You Call Me President." *McCalls*, March 1963, pp. 51–52.

Durslag, Melvin. "Still in Fashion: Small Purses." *TV Guide*, 2, April 1977, pp. 20–22.

Fedler, F., J. Hall, and L. Tanzi. "Popular Songs Emphasize Sex, Deemphasize Romance." *Mass Communication Review* 9 (Spring-Fall 1982): 10–15.

Fernley, Allison, and Paula Maloof. "Yentl." *Film Quarterly* 38 (Spring 1985): 38–46.

Flippo, Chet. "Dolly Parton." *Rolling Stone*, December 11, 1980, pp. 332–39.

Haskell, Molly. "Women and the Silent Comedians." In *Movie Comedy*, edited by Stuart Byron and Elisabeth Weis, pp. 36–40. New York: Grossman, 1977.

Hesbacher, Peter, Nancy Clasby, H. Gerald Clasby and David Berger, "Solo Female Vocalists: Some Shifts in Stature and Alterations in Song," *Popular Music and Society*, 5 (1977): 1–16.

Horowitz, Susan. "Sitcom Domesticus." *Channels*, September/October 1984, pp. 22–23, 50.

"I Love Lucy." *Newsweek*, February 18, 1952, p. 67.

"Image of Woman on Television: A Dialogue." *Journal of Broadcasting* 19 Summer 1975, pp. 289–94.

Ingram, Anne Gayle. "Legal Status of Women in Sports." *Sport Sociology Bulletin* 5 (1976): 30–31.

Karp, Walter, "What Do Women Want?" *Channels* September/October 1984, pp. 17–19.

Kellor, Frances A. "Ethical Value of Sports for Women." *American Physical Education Review* II (1906): 27–35.

Loder, Kurt. "Tina Turner: Sole Survivor." *Rolling Stone*, October 11, 1984, pp. 18–20, 57–60.

"Lucy, Having a Ball at 62." *Ladies Home Journal*, April 1974, pp. 74–78, 150.

McGuigan, Cathleen. "The Sexy Godmother of Rock." *Newsweek*, March 4, 1985, pp. 50–51.

Messenger, Janet G. "Foremothers: Eleanor Holm." *womenSports* 4 July 1977: 15–16.

Norment, Lynn. "Sizzling at Forty-Five." *Ebony*, May 1985, pp. 77–79, 84.

Pally, Marcia. "Kaddish." *Film Comment* 20 (January-February 1984): 49–55.

Poirier, Richard. "Mass Appeal." *New Republic* 173 (August 2 and 9, 1975): 25–28.

Rapoport, Daniel. "Help Wanted: Women Sportswriters." *Parade*, Chicago Sun-Times, December 5, 1976, pp. 17, 19.

Reynolds, Quentin. "Girl Who Lived Again." *Reader's Digest* 65 (October 1954): 50–55.

Rodnitzky, Jerome L. "Songs of Sisterhood: The Music of Women's Liberation." Paper presented to the Popular Culture Association meeting, March 21, 1975, St. Louis, Mo.

Sanders, Ronald. "The American Popular Song." In *Next Year in Jerusalem*, edited by Douglas Villiers, pp. 197–218. New York: Viking Press, 1976.

Seggar, John F., Jeffrey K. Hafen, and Helena Hannonen-Gladden. "Television's Portrayals of Minorities and Women in Drama and Comedy Drama 1971–80." *Journal of Broadcasting* 25 (Summer 1981): 277–88.

Seldes, Gilbert. "Comical Gentlewomen." *Saturday Review*, May 2, 1953, pp. 31–36.

Spitzer, Marian. "The People of Vaudeville," *Saturday Evening Post*, July 12, 1924, pp. 15, 64, 66, 68.

Thomas, Marian. "Women in Television." *Televiser* 1 (Spring 1945): 22.

Waters, Harry F. "A Sex Change in Prime Time." *Newsweek*, January 10, 1983, pp. 72–73.

Index

About the Author

JUNE SOCHEN is Professor of History at Northeastern Illinois University, Chicago, where she teaches courses on U.S. women, including Women in Popular Culture. She also lectures frequently throughout the country on the history of U.S. women.

She is the author and editor of eight books, including textbooks on U.S. women's history: *Herstory: A Record of the American Woman's Past* (second edition, 1981) and *Consecrate Every Day: The Public Lives of Jewish American Women, 1880–1980* (1981).

Professor Sochen holds a B.A. from the University of Chicago and an M.A. and Ph.D. from Northwestern University. She is a member of the American Studies Association.